EASY

Dan McQuillan & Katie Scarlet Eldredge

Open Road Publishing

Open Road Publishing

We offer travel guides to American and foreign locales. Our books tell it like it is, often with an opinionated edge, and our experienced authors always give you all the information you need to have the trip of a lifetime. Write for your free catalog of all our titles.

Open Road Publishing
P.O. Box 284, Cold Spring Harbor, NY 11724
www.openroadguides.com
E-mail: Jopenroad@aol.com

ABOUT THE AUTHORS

Dan McQuillan is the author of Open Road's *Ireland Guide* and *Scotland Guide*; he makes his home in Centennial, Colorado. Katie Scarlet Eldredge is a freelance travel writer who has updated a number of books for Open Road, including our Arizona and Colorado guides. She lives in Aurora, Illinois.

TABLE OF CONTENTS

Maps

DUBLIN *MADE EASY*

INTRODUCTION

With slightly over one million people in its greater metropolitan area, **Dublin** is the largest city on the Emerald Isle and has been an important seaport for nearly a millennium. The **River Liffey** is the major waterway in Dublin, and it bisects the city from east to west.

Dublin is situated perfectly for walking tours – the vast majority of the best sights are within easy walking distance from the central part of Dublin. Cultural, architectural, and historical sights and sounds are present on nearly every corner and around every bend. Museums, art galleries, historic sites, marvelous shopping, and quiet sunsets all vie for your time and attention.

As you follow the walks we have outlined in this guide, we'll make sure that you don't miss the best that Dublin has to offer. Well – the best is the people, of course. But we've suggested the best sights Dublin has to offer. Along the way we'll point out some superb dining establishments and provide you with the names of a few great places to stay.

So – lace up your shoes, stretch a bit before you head out, and look forward to a few wonderful, fun-filled and interesting days ahead of you! This handy little pocket guide to Dublin will make your visit enjoyable, memorable – *and easy*!

DUBLIN'S BEST SIGHTS

Dublin is a comfortable city to walk in: there are many tree-lined streets, occasional parks, and interesting sights within easy distance from one another. Dublin is not very hilly, so your walks will be a pleasure!

Following are Dublin's top sights – the ones you definitely want to see while you are here:

Book of Kells: Housed at Trinity College. Ancient monks hand-illustrated the Bible's four gospels over 1,100 years ago. And now it's on display for you to see.

Chester Beatty Library & Gallery of Oriental Art: This is an incredible museum. Located behind Dublin Castle, it's definitely worth spending a few minutes to visit.

Christchurch Cathderal: The two finest cathedrals in Ireland are located in Dublin. St. Patrick's is one, Christchurch is the other.

Dublin Writer's Museum: This is a museum that is devoted to Ireland's most beloved writers.

General Post Office (GPO): There aren't many cities where I'd suggest going to see the main post office. But the GPO has played such an important role in Irish history, it's a must.

Grafton Street: This pedestrian shopping street provides ample opportunity for shopping and people watching.

Guinness Brewery: Visit the brewery that made Dublin famous. The tour no longer takes you back into the brewery itself, but provides a video tour.

Hugh Lane Municipal Gallery of Modern Art: Another fine art gallery in Dublin. This one focuses on contemporary art.

National Gallery of Ireland: The National Gallery is the best art gallery in Ireland, and is well worth a visit.

National Museum: If you see only one museum in Ireland, this should be the one.

Phoenix Park: Lots of greenery, cricket games, polo matches, ducks and ponds, a fabulous zoo, and people-watching.

St. Michan's Church: This 300+ year old church is an interesting visit, especially with a trip to the cellars to see the mummified remains of former parishioners.

St. Patrick's Cathedral: As impressive as Christchurch Cathedral, but different too.

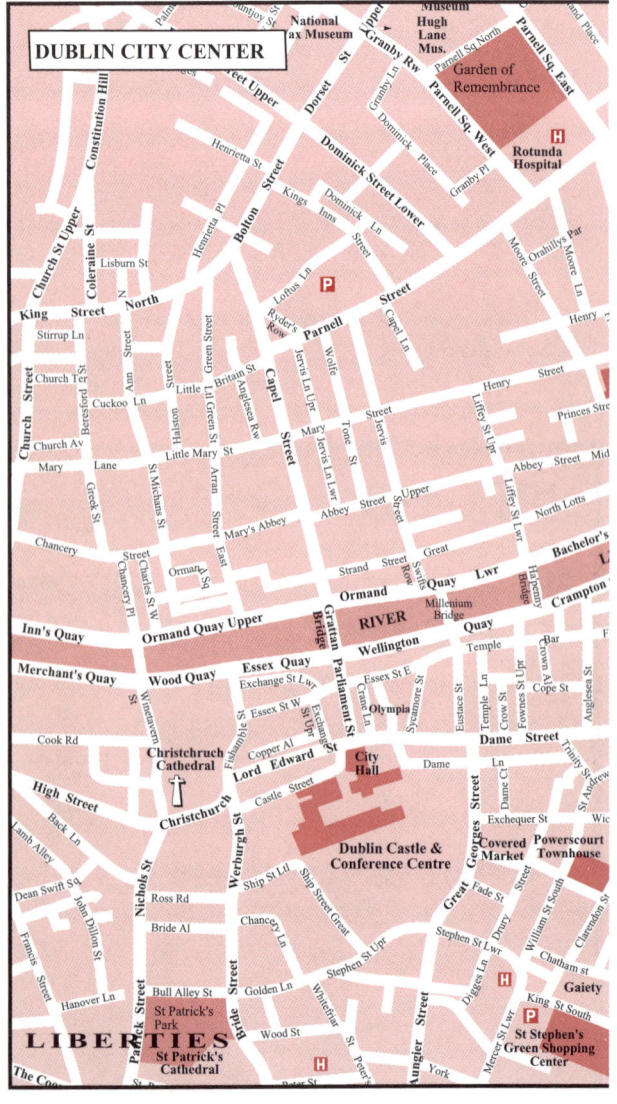

DUBLIN CITY CENTER

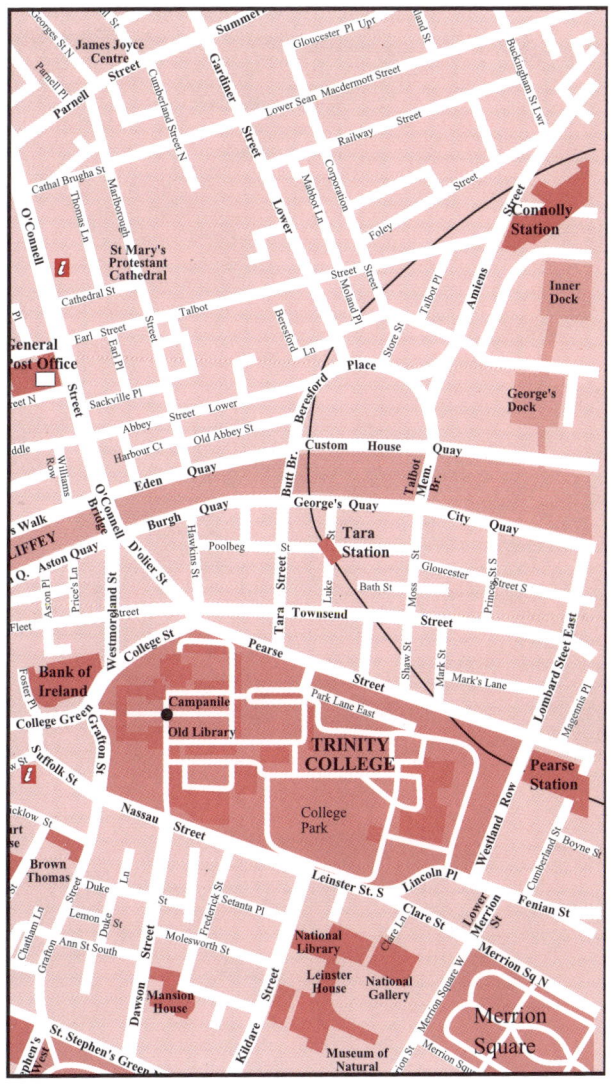

1. WALKS

Top Dublin Sights Walk

If you only have one day to spend in Dublin, this is the walk for you. We will hit the major attractions Dublin has to offer in this walk. **Featured Sights**: St. Patrick's Cathedral, Christchurch Cathedral, The Book of Kells (Trinity College), Grafton Street, the National Museum of Ireland, Guinness Storehouse, Phoenix Park.

Begin at **St. Patrick's Cathedral** on Patrick Street. Dublin is home to two of Ireland's most impressive cathedrals, and this is one of them. Christchurch Cathedral, our next stop on this walk, is the other. Originally built outside Dublin's city walls, St. Patrick's earned itself the nickname "the church of the people," while Christchurch, which was built inside the city walls, was often called "the church of the government."

Physically, St. Patrick's is impressive. It is the largest church in Ireland; the interior is as long as a football field. As with any other cathedral, you will expect to see beautiful stained glass windows, and you will not be disappointed.

There are many historical artifacts on display in St. Patrick's Cathedral. One of the more impressive is the "**Door of Reconciliation**" found in the northeast section of the cathedral. In 1472 two powerful men in Ireland were warring: the Earl of Kildare and the Earl of Ormond. Hotly pursued, the latter sought sanctuary in the Chapter House and a standoff followed. The Earl of Kildare, tired of war, chopped a hole in the door and, as an act of reconciliation, thrust his arm through the hole and grasped the hand of his enemy, ending the war.

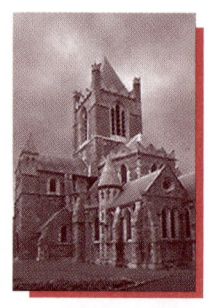

From here proceed to Christchurch Cathedral. Exit St. Patrick's and go north on

Patrick Street, which becomes Nicholas Street after a few blocks. Christchurch Cathedral is one block north on Nicholas Street, on the left (it'll be hard to miss!).

Top Sights Walk

Christchurch Cathedral is just as impressive as St. Patrick's and certainly deserves a visit. This cathedral was built in 1038 for the Norse King Sitric Silkenbeard (is that a great name, or what?). Originally a wooden structure, a major renovation was undertaken between 1173 and 1220 where the wood was replaced by stone. In 1831 the cathedral received a final facelift, and was redone in the Gothic style you see today.

Among the other relics you will find in Christchurch Cathedral is the effigy of **Strongbow**. His actual tomb used to be housed in the Cathedral, but was destroyed 400 years ago when part of the roof caved in. However, the heart (yes, the actual heart) of St. Lawrence O'Toole is preserved in a metal casket at the east end of the cathedral. He was the Archbishop at the time of Strongbow's invasion.

Take Christchurch Place east and follow its curve north. Go east on Lord Edward Street, (which becomes Dame Street, which becomes College Green) for several blocks. You'll run right into Trinity College.

Without a doubt, the most important holding at **Trinity College** is the **Book of Kells**, the ornately illustrated four Gospels written by the monks of Kells Monastery in the 9th century. The title pages of each of the four gospels are especially elaborate. There are also many scenes depicting Christ's life, including His temptation and arrest.

Restaurant Tip

OLIVER ST. JOHN GOGARTY

58-59 Fleet Street (from Dame Street go north on Anglesea Street, then right onto Fleet Street).
Tel (01) 288-4707.

The best place in Dublin to sample "pub grub." Crowded, noisy atmosphere. Most nights there is traditional Irish music in the bar upstairs, and there is often music on the first floor too.

Top
Sights
Walk

The Book of Kells is kept in a glass case in a room with muted lighting. Two gospels are shown at a time and the pages are turned daily.

As you enter the room, there are also cases along the walls (which you walk past while in line) that contain other ancient books, including the **Book of Durrow**, which was written in 675, and is the earliest surviving decorated book of the Gospels. The **Book of Armagh** is another you'll see, and it was written in 807.

If you're like me, you'll leave wishing you could see more of the beautifully ornamented pages. Never fear – the gift shop associated with the Book of Kells offers a picture book with all the pictures from the Book of Kells shown in vibrant color.

After you view of the Book of Kells, you are treated to a fascinating stroll through the lavish **Long Room of the Old Library** on your way out. This impressive room is over 200 feet long and 40 feet wide. For nearly 200 years, Trinity College has been receiving a copy of every book published in Ireland and England, and many of them are on display here in the Old Library.

Included in the holdings of the library are first editions of some of Shakespeare's works, as well as copies of the original printing of the *Proclamation of 1916* (Ireland's equivalent of the Declaration of Independence); look for it as soon as you enter the Long Hall – usually displayed on your left. In addition, there is a wonderful 15th-century harp on display. It is in remarkable condition, from its oak and willow wood-work to its 29 brass strings. Legend has it that the harp once belonged to the Irish warrior/poet/king Brian Boru; however, scholars point out that Brian was born some 500 years before the harp was made (spoilsports!).

Exit Trinity College through its front gates and turn left – to the south. Cross Nassau Street and you will find yourself on Grafton Street.

Top Sights Walk

As you leave Trinity College and head for Grafton Street, don't miss the **Molly Malone statue**, which sits at the intersection of Grafton and Suffolk Streets, at the north end of Grafton Street. Don't miss this Dublin icon.

Grafton Street is so full of life and Irish culture it is truly a treat. My favorite part about Grafton Street are the *buskers*, street entertainers, who routinely perform here. From jugglers to gymnasts, to singers and small bands, there is always some show to see! Don't rush here. Stroll from busker to busker, slipping into an occasional shop or two along the way.

Restaurant Tip

PASTA FRESCA
2-4 Chatham Street (near Westbury Hotel off Grafton Street). Tel. (01) 475-2597.

The atmosphere in this Italian restaurant is light and cheerful (almost *fun*). Their main claim to fame is that they make their own pasta fresh daily. Whether that is the reason or not, the food is exceptionally good!

Leave Grafton Street from its south end and turn left (east) onto St. Stephen's Green North. Two blocks down turn left (north) onto Kildare Street. The National Museum of Ireland will be on your right.

If you only have time to see one museum while in Dublin, this should be the one. The **National Museum** of Ireland will lead you through the history of Ireland from the Bronze Age (2200 BC to 700 BC) to present day. One thing somewhat unique about this museum is that the plaques about the exhibits are written in Gaelic as well as in English.

One of the most interesting exhibits is entitled *Ar Thóir na Saoirse*, which means "The Road to Independence." This exhibit deals with the major personalities and events that took place between 1916 and 1922 in Ireland's struggle for independence.

| Top Sights Walk | The museum gives you a grand tour of Ireland's birth, history and destiny. Although the museum isn't large, there are many exhibits that will help you gain greater insights into Ireland's past. |

Once finished at the museum, you can either take a bus (bus #123 from Dame Street) or walk (about 15 minutes) to get to our next stop on the tour: the Guinness Storehouse.

A trip to Ireland would not be complete without a pint of their world-famous Guinness beer. And what better place to have one than at the **Guinness Storehouse** itself? The popular Guinness Storehouse is an amazing 60-acre compound that produces an unbelievable four million pints of the dark brew per day! An audiovisual presentation of the brewery's history is available in the **Hop Store**, after which guests are treated to a complimentary sample of the beer.

Beware, however, that the tour isn't inexpensive. At 14 per adult and 5 for children, it is the most expensive tourist site in Ireland. If you are traveling as a family, there is a family ticket for 30, which helps limit the cost (covers two adults and four children under 18 years).

For our final stop on this tour, you will want to find another bus (bus #s 37, 38 or 39.) to take you to Phoenix Park.

Beautiful **Phoenix Park** is not named for the mythological bird that rises from the ashes, but rather from the Irish words *fionn uisce* (clear water) that sounds like "phoenix" in English. The park is a stunning 1,700 acres and is the largest in Europe. It is more than just trees, grass, ponds and lakes (although it has all those things); it also boasts a zoo, polo grounds, a medieval fortress (Ashtown Castle), and cricket, football and hurling fields. You could easily spend an entire day here, so plan your day accordingly.

See pages 22-23 for more details on this wonderful park.

Gardens & Parks Walk

Featured Sights: Iveagh Gardens, St. Stephen's Green, Merrion Square, Garden of Remembrance, Phoenix Park.

No Dublin adventure is complete until you have seen its parks. Dubliners choose to live in the city, but it is clear from their extensive, exquisite parks that they have not forgotten their roots.

From the southwest corner of St. Stephen's Green, walk south on Harcourt Street and turn left onto Clonmel Street. Iveagh Gardens' entrance is tucked away off to the left.

Iveagh Gardens are a little harder to find than some of the other parks in Dublin, but it is worth the effort. This eleven-acre garden is on the small side for Dublin standards but, possibly because of its size, it is much less frequented than some of Dublin's major parks. The other gardens on this walk are often packed with tourists, parents and their children, joggers, and business people taking a break, but this park is where you go for some peace and quiet.

Aside from the solitude it provides, Iveagh Gardens also has some other wonderful features. It is graced with several fountains and a rose garden that takes up about a quarter of an acre. There is also a hedge maze, although you probably will not have a problem finding your way out unless you happen to be a toddler (it is only about a foot and a half tall).

Exit Iveagh Gardens through the same entrance you came in. Walk north on Harcourt Street to get to St. Stephen's Green. Enter the park at the corner of St. Stephen's Green West and St. Stephen's Green South.

St. Stephen's Green, at 22 acres, is twice the size of Iveagh Gardens. It is so large that even though it is surrounded on all sides by busy streets, once in the middle of the park you can

Gardens & Parks Walk

hardly hear the traffic. This park has a lot to offer and you could easily spend a couple of hours here.

As you enter at the southwest corner of the garden there is a map of the park on the gate to your right. Included in the park's features are two ponds, a playground, and a bandstand. There is also a garden for the blind where visitors are encouraged to feel the different textures of the plants.

Exit the garden from its northwest corner, and as you leave there are a few things to notice. First, at this point in the walk you may be getting hungry or itching for a shopping break. One of the best places in Dublin to find the cure for both of these ailments is **Grafton Street**. As you exit the park look straight across the street and you will see it.

Grafton Street is a pedestrian street lined with shops, restaurants, and cafes. Chances are also good that you will see a number of street performers doing their best to make memories for tourists. It really is a fun thing to see and should not be missed.

After you see Grafton Street, walk east on St. Stephen's Green North. Continue walking east on St. Stephen's Green North, which becomes Merrion Row. Turn left onto Merrion Street Upper. Enter Merrion Park about a block and a half down on your right.

As you stroll down Merrion Street, be sure to notice the **door knockers** on the brightly colored Georgian mansion doors; you will see intricate lions, tigers and bears (oh my!), as well as other designs.

Merrion Square, sometimes called Archbishop Ryan Park, is the next stop on our walk. This is another smallish (11-acre), quiet park. Merrion Square is more overgrown than the others on our walk. There are open grassy areas in this park, but the most memorable parts are the many paths that wend through canopies created by the trees and plants. It is on these trails especially that you are likely to feel like you are the only one

Gardens & Parks Walk

Restaurant Tip

RESTAURANT PATRICK GUILBAUD
21 Merrion St. Tel. (01) 676-4192

If you want to dine at *the* restaurant in Ireland, this is it. It is the first restaurant in Ireland to be awarded a second Michelin star, and it is well deserved. The restaurant is housed in an old Georgian home that has been exquisitely renovated. And the food is marvelous; you will love everything about your visit.

in the park. Take some time to wander through and feel the peace it has to offer.

Merrion Square dates back to 1762 and some of Ireland's most esteemed and important citizens called the fine Georgian townhouses around Merrion Square home. Some of these famous residents include Oscar Wilde's parents (Number 1), W.B. Yeats (Numbers 52 and 82), and the Duke of Wellington (Number 24 Upper Merrion Street). Many of the homes have plaques near their front doors identifying their famous former inhabitants.

If the plaques outside these townhouses do not satisfy your curiosity about them, you should stop into Number Twenty-Nine Fitzwilliam Street, just east of Merrion Square on (where else?) Fitzwilliam Street. The National Museum of Ireland and the Electricity Supply Board have combined their talents and funds to restore Number Twenty-Nine as it likely was in the late 18th century: the home of a middle-class family. Great attention to detail has been given to everything from the woodwork to the furnishings, the walls and ceilings. You truly feel as though you have stepped back in time when you visit.

On Saturdays and Sundays along the sidewalks outside Merrion Square, local artists can be found selling their work. There is something here to fit every taste: landscapes, animals, abstract art, and portraits — you name it, they sell it. There are so many pieces to be seen it feels like an outdoor museum. This is also a great place to chat with the local artists.

To get to our next stop on this walk, the Garden of Remembrance,

<table>
<tr><td>Gardens & Parks Walk</td><td>you can either walk (it'll be about one mile), or hop on a bus – any bus numbered 10, 11, 11A, 11B, 12, 13, 14, 16, 16A, 19A, 22, 22A, 36. Get off at Parnell Square.</td></tr>
</table>

Your bus will probably head up O'Connell Street. Two blocks after you cross the River Liffey, be sure to look out your window and take notice of the **Spire of Dublin**. The Irish tend to nickname their monuments, and this one is no exception. The Spire of Dublin is often called, among other things, *the Stiffy by the Liffey*, *the Pointless Point*, and (my favorite) *the Stiletto in the Ghetto*.

The Garden of Remembrance was built in 1966 to commemorate the fiftieth anniversary of the Easter Rising of 1916, which led to Ireland's independence. The garden is quite small, but it is meant to be a memorial to those who gave their lives for Ireland's freedom. (Think of it as Ireland's version of the Minuteman statue in Lexington, Massachusetts.)

While visiting the Garden of Remembrance, be sure and take a few minutes to consider the statue that looks like children chasing geese and making them fly away. It represents the legendary **Children of Lir**. Legend has it that the children of Lir were turned into geese by their stepmother. They remained geese for 900 years until Christianity came to Ireland, at which point they returned to their human forms.

To reach the last stop on this walk, hop on another bus (numbers 37, 38 or 39) and make your way toward Phoenix Park.

As you enter **Phoenix Park**, keep an eye out for the big white house near the edge of Phoenix Park; it is the house of Ireland's President. Phoenix Park originally opened to the public 250 years ago. It is the last spot on our walk, because if you have the time and the desire you might take a whole day to see this park.

There is something for everyone at Phoenix Park. If you are traveling with children, they will no doubt enjoy the **Dublin**

Zoo, found on the park grounds. It has a wide variety of animals and a place for children to get "up close and personal" with less exotic (and much safer!) animals such as rabbits, chickens, and goats.

If you enjoy sports, Phoenix Park won't let you down. Just past the zoo are the **Polo Grounds**. Whether or not you understand the rules of the game (I don't), it is fun to watch the practices and games. The horses are magnificent and it is a treat to see them wheeling and charging.

On the far south side of the park are the **Dublin Dueling Grounds**, where the gentility of Dublin came to shoot at each other hundreds of years ago. Today this area hosts far more civilized hostility and competition in the form of hurling, cricket, and football.

Churches & Cathedrals Walk

Featured Sights: St. Michan's Church, Christchurch Cathedral, Royal Chapel of Dublin Castle, St. Patrick's Cathedral.

Dublin's population is 92% Catholic, and so visiting some of their impressive churches and cathedrals is a must. Most of these churches, however, now belong to the Church of Ireland.

Let's start our walk at St. Michan's Church, a few blocks north of the River Liffey.. To get here, take O'Connell Street north to Henry Street, turn left (west) and walk about ten minutes (four blocks) along Henry Street/Mary Street/Mary's Lane to Church Street. Turn right and St. Michan's will be on your left.

St. Michan's Church was originally built in 1095 as a Viking parish church, and was the only church north of the River Liffey for 500 years. It was rebuilt to its present state in 1686, and has had several renovations since then. As you walk around, notice the beautiful woodwork throughout the church.

Legend has it that Handel played St. Michan's magnificent 18th-century organ while composing *The Messiah*. (This is the Irish equivalent of "George Washington Slept here.")

From here we walk south on Church Street to Inns Quay. Turn left and go about a block to the Richmond Bridge and cross the River Liffey, then continue south on Winetavern Street for one more block. Christchurch Cathedral will be on your left on Christchurch Place.

Christchurch Cathedral is a must-see in Dublin. The most noticeable aspects of the interior of this cathedral are the intricate stonework and the elegant stained glass windows. If you are lucky, there might even be an organist performing on the day you visit, which certainly adds to the ambience.

In about the middle of the cathedral, on the right, be sure to notice two interesting previous inhabitants of the cathedral: a mummified cat and rat. They apparently participated in a deadly game of "cat and mouse" in days gone by. The rat raced into an organ pipe with the cat hot on its tail. The cat became lodged in the pipe and both the dinner and the diner perished.

The cathedral has a crypt in the basement that is worth at least a glance. The crypt dates from the late twelfth century, making it the oldest structure in Dublin; it houses many historical artifacts, including a stock from 1670. Law-breakers were sometimes locked in these, where they were pelted with fruit and vegetables.

While you are at Christchurch Cathedral, you might want to pop over to **Dublinia**. It is across the street from the Cathedral, but there is an enclosed walkway going over the road that connects the two. Dublinia is a small, creative museum that helps visitors understand what it would have been like to live in medieval Dublin. As you wander through the museum you suddenly find yourself aboard a Viking ship, then moments later you are in a merchant's home. Dublinia is certainly worth the time to visit.

To get to our next stop, go east on Christchurch Place. Christchurch Place curves north, but we will continue east onto Castle Street. One block down is Dublin Castle.

This is where the **Royal Chapel of Dublin Castle** is housed, an elegant little church with beautiful oak panels and lovely stained-glass windows. Notice that on these stained-glass windows and on the oak around the balcony are the coats of arms of 150 English viceroys.

The Royal Chapel was completed in 1814 based on the designs of Francis Johnston. It served as an Anglican Church for over 125 years. However, in 1943, the Catholic Church began using it for their services and they continue to do so today.

From here we will backtrack a little and go west on Castle Street. Turn left (south) after two blocks onto Werburgh Street, which becomes Bride Street after a couple of blocks. Turn right onto Bull Alley and then left (south) onto Patrick Street. As you head down the street to St. Patrick's Cathedral (which will be on your left), notice the well-kept grounds you are passing.

St. Patrick's Cathedral was founded in 1191, but its history goes back much further. Local historians will tell you that this is perhaps the oldest Christian site in Dublin. Tradition says that it was on this spot that St. Patrick performed baptisms. St. Patrick's is the largest cathedral in Ireland. Its west clock tower and the spire atop it are, combined, nearly 250 feet high. As you walk in, you might feel like the front of the cathedral is about a football field's length away from you. You would be right; the interior of the cathedral is 300 feet long.

Jonathan Swift was dean of St. Patrick's Cathedral for over thirty years, from 1713 to 1745. His pulpit is still on display here, along with various other things that belonged to him.

Museums & Art Galleries Walk

Featured Sights: National Museum of Ireland, National Gallery of Ireland, Royal Hospital Kilmainham/ Irish Museum of Modern Art, Kilmainham Gaol Historical Museum.

One of the most impressive things about the museums and art galleries in Dublin is that they are free. Dubliners really do want tourists to get a taste of their history and talents, and so they make the display of these as easily accessible as possible.

We will begin at the most logical place, the National Museum of Ireland. You can find that by walking to the south end of Grafton Street and turning left at St. Stephen's Green. Walk two blocks to Kildare Street, then turn left again and the museum is about 200 yards down on your right.

 Much like the Smithsonian, there are multiple locations for the **National Museum of Ireland**. Start at the **Archeology and History** building, found on Kildare Street. Be sure to take notice of the building itself. There are marble floors, brass railings, intricate crown moldings, and beautiful carved wood doors.

This campus of the Museum of Ireland will take you through Ireland's history from the Bronze Age (2200 BC to 700 BC) to the present. One of the highlights of this museum is a **replica of the Newgrange passage grave** in County Meath. The actual cross-shaped tomb, about an hour north of Dublin, is nearly 5,000 years old and is wonderfully preserved. If you can't make the drive to see the original, be sure to take a look at the replica here.

Exit the museum onto Kildare Street and go south. Take your first left onto Merrion Row and then your first left again onto Merrion Street Upper. On your left you will see the Natural History Museum.

Museums & Art Galleries Walk

Restaurant Tip

LATCHFORDS BISTRO
99-100 Lower Baggot Street (stay on Merrion Row, which becomes Baggot Street). Tel. (01) 676-0784.

This family-run French/Italian bistro offers a warm, comfortable atmosphere topped only by the excellent cuisine and impressive presentation of the meal. Popular with the locals.

The Natural History Museum is comprised of four floors crammed full of animals and insects. The first floor is dedicated to animals found in Ireland, the most notable of which is a huge skeleton of the now extinct Giant Irish Deer, which looks like it was about as big as a moose. There are also the skeletons of two whales suspended from the ceiling.

The second floor houses big animals such as tigers, elephants, and lions. This is one museum that your kids will not be rushing you to get through; you may have to drag *them* out!

Our next stop, the National Gallery of Ireland, is right next door (north on Merrion Street) to the Natural History museum.

It you are hoping to see works by Irish painters on your trip to Dublin, the **National Gallery of Ireland** will not disappoint you. Probably every major Irish artist, along with many not-so-major ones, are represented here. You will also find works by Rembrandt, Degas, El Greco, Monet, Reynolds, Rubens, Titian, Van Dyck, and others.

The gallery also has a beautiful ballroom, complete with four chandeliers, where they hold lectures. There might be one of interest to you on the day you visit. Be sure to check it out.

To get to our next two sights, you will need to catch a bus (unless you are up for a very long walk). Your bus will take you west to Kilmainham Lane where you will find our next museum.

The splendid building that houses the **Royal Hospital Kilmainham/Irish Museum of Modern Art** was once a soldier's hospital. After the establishment of the Irish Free State in

1922, the building was closed and fell into disrepair. A fifteen-year, $30 million renovation project has paid handsome dividends - the building is once again a grand structure.

The Irish Museum of Modern Art (IMMA) is comprised of four galleries surrounding a large and lovely courtyard. An eclectic array of twentieth-century art is exhibited throughout the museum, and there always seems to be a one-man show or an exhibit going on. The Banqueting Hall is now the site of frequent concerts and special events. Perhaps the prettiest room is the chapel, which has rich wood paneling and a Baroque ceiling. This grand structure is worth a visit even if you have no interest in modern art.

Leave the IMMA through the back of the courtyard. Follow the long dirt road away from the museum. Be sure to enjoy the view of the river off to your right. After about a five-minute walk, you will come to Inchicore Road. Cross it and you will see our next stop.

Step into the darker side of Ireland's past at the **Kilmainham Gaol Historical Museum**. This restored prison, built in 1796 and used until 1924, gives visitors a peek into the terrible conditions endured by Irish patriots awaiting execution or a one-way ticket to Australia. Among the most infamous acts performed here was the execution of those who penned their names to the Proclamation of the Republic in 1916 (the Irish equivalent of the Declaration of Independence).

But patriots were not the only prisoners here; children as young as seven served sentences at Kilmainham jail. At some points in the jail's history, almost half of the prisoners were women.

Restaurant Tip

NUMBER 10
10 Fitzwilliam Street Lower (east of and parallel to Merrion Street Upper). Tel. (01) 676-1367.

Arguably one of the finest dining establishments in Dublin. You'll find an open fire, accentuated by the crystal and linen on the tables, excellent service, and first-rate food – all in all, an elegant and graceful dining experience.

During the Irish Potato Famine of 1845 through 1848 people were actually committing crimes so they would be sent to Kilmainham Jail, where they would at least have something to eat. To discourage this, the jailors began feeding the prisoners a subsistence diet, just enough to keep them alive.

North of the Liffey Walk

Featured Sights: O'Connell Street, the General Post Office (GPO), Henry Street, the Garden of Remembrance, Dublin Writer's Museum.

It seems that most of Dublin's sites are located south of the Liffey, but there are a few sights north of the Liffey that you should be sure to see on your trip to Dublin.

Begin at the intersection of O'Connell Street where it crosses the River Liffey. As you head north across the bridge, Daniel O'Connell himself (or at least his statue) stands to welcome you to O'Connell Street. This is one of the most important streets in Dublin.

O'Connell Street was named after Daniel O'Connell, one of Ireland's most revered individuals. He was a former Dublin Mayor and winner of Catholic emancipation. The wide central island is punctuated by large trees and statues of Irish greats: Daniel O'Connell (of course), William Smith O'Brien (leader of one of Ireland's many rebellions against British authority), James Larkin (a historic union leader), Sir John Gay (newspaper editor), and others.

The silver, pointed tower called the **Spire of Dublin**, rising 393 feet above the street, is hard to miss! It was completed in early 2003 on the site of the former Nelson Pillar, which was a tribute to British Admiral Nelson. In March of 1966 Irish loyalists, who resented the pillar's lofty position in the city, blew it up, reducing the pillar to a pile of rubble.

| North of the Liffey Walk | *The next stop on this tour is the General Post Office (GPO). It is at the intersection of O'Connell Street and Henry Street.* |

There are not very many cities in the world where we would recommend a visit to the post office, but Dublin's General Post Office (GPO) has played such an important role in the history of the city, you really should at least take notice of it. It was from the seized GPO that Irish rebel leaders proclaimed their message of a new republic. The ensuing battle destroyed most of the area around O'Connell Street. In fact, some of the GPO's massive stone pillars still bear the scars of flying bullets.

The words of the proclamation read by those rebel leaders on that fateful Easter are inscribed in a green marble plaque in the GPO. All the men who signed this proclamation also, in effect, signed their death warrants; they were taken to Kilmainham Jail and executed.

Next we will go to Henry Street, which is on the north side of the GPO.

Henry Street is a pedestrian shopping street. It has a similar feel to Grafton Street, which has largely replaced it as *the* shopping street in Dublin. Henry Street is still, however, crowded with people most hours of the day and evening.

About half a block west of O'Connell Street on the right is a large tile mosaic on the walkway that announces the entrance to **Moore Street**, which has for generations been the fruit, vegetable, and flower market of Dublin. It is a fun place to go, as it is full of all sorts of colorful sights and cheerful sounds.

Continue north on Moore Street until you hit Parnell Street onto which you will turn right (east). Half a block down, turn left (north) onto Parnell Square West and then right (east) onto Parnell Square North. Here you will see the entrance to the Garden of Remembrance.

The **Garden of Remembrance** is very small by Irish standards, but it is meant more as a memorial than a park. It was built on the fiftieth anniversary of the 1916 Easter rebellion, which led to Ireland's independence from Britain, and serves as a memorial to those who gave their lives that Ireland might be free.

The square features an ornamental pond in the form of a crucifix, and the setting is serene and peaceful.

Now we move onto our last stop of this tour, the Dublin Writer's Museum. It is right across the street from The Garden of Remembrance.

Ireland has always loved its writers and poets, and this museum honors them. The **Dublin Writer's Museum** is one of the most elegant, tasteful, and well thought-out museums in Ireland. It is housed in an exquisitely restored Georgian home. The Gorham Library on the first floor houses the permanent exhibits. It is here that paintings, memorabilia, letters, and photographs immortalize such famed Irish authors as Samuel Beckett, George Bernard Shaw, Jonathan Swift, and Oscar Wilde.

Shopping Walk

Featured Sights: Francis Street, Powerscourt Centre, St. Stephen's Green Shopping Centre, Grafton Street, O'Connell Street, Moore Street.

Start on Dublin's Antique Row – also known as Francis Street. To get to Francis Street, start at Trinity College. Walk west on Dame Street, which becomes Lord Edward Street, which becomes High Street. Once you reach High Street, turn left on Francis Street and you're on Antique Row.

Shopping Walk

Francis Street is known far and wide for its interesting and intriguing **antiques stores**. Would you like a suit of armor? How about a 17th century button? Been searching for a looking glass from the Louis XIV era?

All these and much more can be found here. Many of the shops have two things in common: fascinating antiques and a lack of space. Most are jammed full of artifacts.

O'Sullivan's Antiques at 44 Francis Street is one of the largest stores on Antique Row. You'll think you have walked into a museum of antique furniture and bric-a-brac, but the main difference is that you can purchase anything you see here. O'Sullivan's is easy to spot – its large Kelly green building with awnings is very prominent. **Fleury's Antiques** also has a prominent presence on Francis Street, as well as throughout Ireland. But don't overlook some of the smaller stores – including **Forsythe** and **Odeon** antiques. These stores have just as much charm and perhaps even more character than some of the larger stores on Francis Street.

From the south end of Francis Street, turn left on The Coombe. Follow that as it turns into Kevin Street, until it dead ends at Aungier Street. Turn left, then after about a block on your right, turn right onto St. Stephen's Street Upper. Follow that one block to Williams Street, and turn left, where you'll find the Powerscourt Centre shopping mall.

Powerscourt mixes the old and the new – in more ways than one. Over forty shops are packed into this former 18th century Georgian mansion. The shops are as eclectic as you'd expect, from jewelry to upscale clothing to antiques. You'll find a number of casual restaurants here also, including a vegetarian place (suitably named **Café Fresh**) and coffee shops. For *Lord of the Rings* fans, you might want to check out the jewelry store called **Gollum's Precious**!

Back out on Williams Street, backtrack slightly to St. Stephen's Street Lower, turn left and merge onto King Street. At the corner of King and Grafton Streets, you'll find the St. Stephen's Green

Grafton Street

Blarney Castle

Christchurch Cathedtral

Glendalough

Ivy-covered red door, one of many colorful doors in Dublin

Trinity College, home of the Book of Kells

O'Connell Bridge

The Dublin Spire

Shopping Centre, across from the northwest corner of St. Stephen's Green.

Shopping Walk

St. Stephen's Green Shopping Centre has a variety of stores here, with glitzy stores and signs, amidst a sort of faux Victorian feel. **Dunne's**, one of the larger chain department stores in Ireland, is the anchor store here, and has a very large presence. The shopping center is always a hive of activity, and is well used by Dubliners and tourists alike. Entertainment such as puppet shows, bands, and various other groups are also featured throughout the day.

Now let's get you to Dublin's Number 1 shopping district – **Grafton Street**. Grafton Street is a hodgepodge of upscale stores, buskers (street entertainers), pubs and most anything else you can imagine. This pedestrianized street offers many shops and sights to grab your attention. Jewelry stores vie for your attention along with upscale clothing stores such as Marks & Spencer and Korkeys, and a number of restaurants from Bewleys to McDonalds (they're everywhere!). As mentioned in earlier walks, Grafton Street is just pure fun, whether you like shopping, people watching, or street entertainment. The energy and vibrancy on Grafton Street is higher than just about any place else in Ireland.

When you reach the north end of Grafton Street, continue north in front of Trinity College, then bear slightly left onto Westmoreland Street, which becomes O'Connell Street once you cross the Liffey.

O'Connell Street was the place to be in Victorian Dublin; it then fell into disrepair, but is now renovated. Though there is still some work to be completed, O'Connell Street is reclaiming its long-lost luster. Restaurants, department stores, clothing and jewelry stores now pack its buildings along the wide thoroughfare. **Clery's**, another of Ireland's major department stores, is one of the main tenants now. Today you'll typically find many shoppers, commuters (buses home in on O'Connell Street) and a few street entertainers.

From O'Connell Street near the General Post Office (GPO), slip onto Henry Street heading west.

Shopping Walk

You'll find a host of interesting shops, most not so upscale as those on O'Connell or Grafton Streets. But the real treasure here is **Moore Street**, about a block down on your right.

Moore Street hosts an open-air market where the raucous voices of vendors can be heard, vying for your attention with their fruits, vegetables and flowers. Watch for the large tile mosaic on the walkway that announces the entrance to Moore Street, then enjoy the sights and sounds, whether you purchase anything or not.

2. SIGHTS

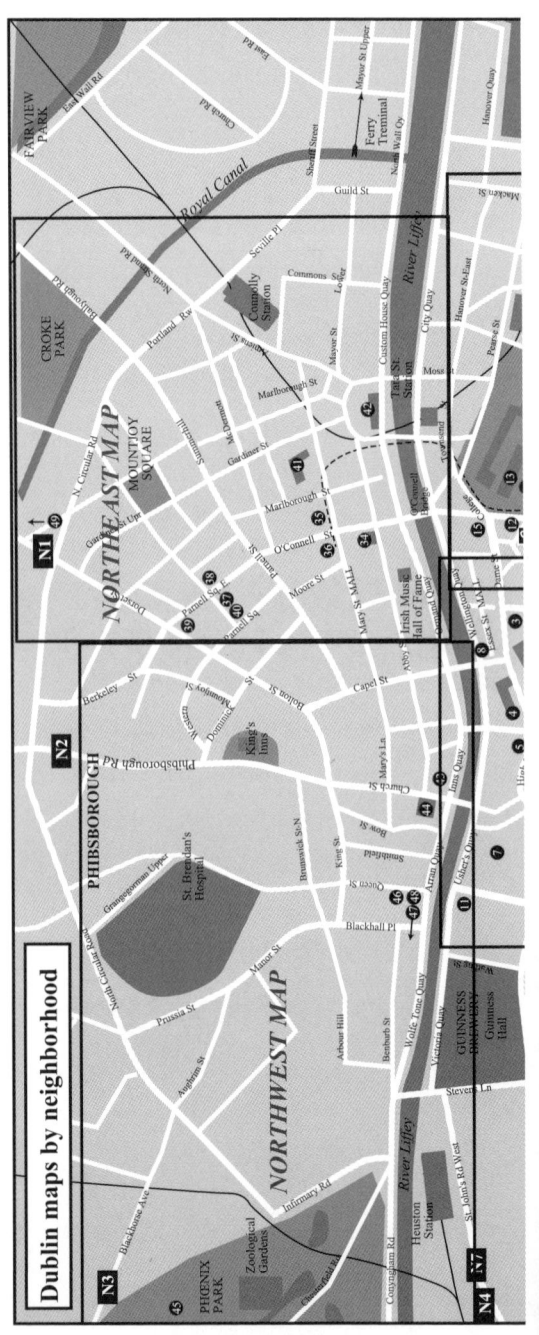

Dublin maps by neighborhood

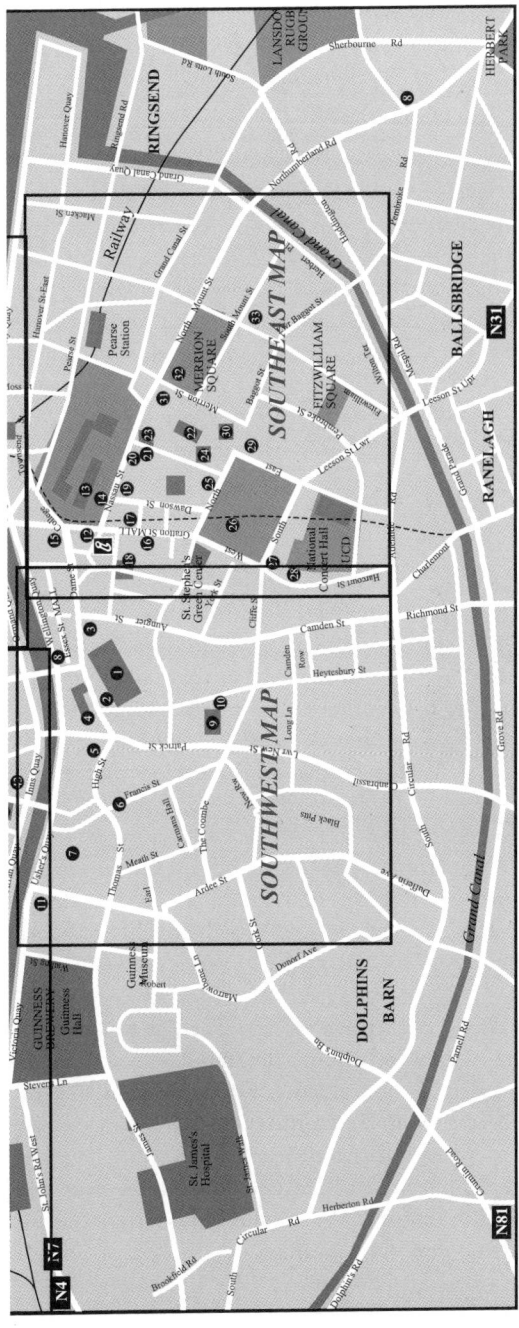

South of the Liffey – Temple Bar District

The **River Liffey** is the lifeblood, the main artery of Dublin. Two of the most beautiful evening sights are along the banks of the river: The Custom House and the Four Courts offer gorgeous lighted views at night. Most addresses are described as either north or south of the River Liffey. A dozen bridges span its girth in Dublin. The most familiar and popular are the **O'Connell Bridge** and the **Ha'penny Bridge**. In this section, I've provided the best the Temple Bar District has to offer.

1. Dublin Castle

Castle Street, open Monday through Saturday 10am to 5pm, Saturdays, Sundays and bank holidays from 2pm until 5pm. Last admission is 15 minutes before closing. Admission is €4.50 for adults, €3.50 for seniors and students and €2 for children. Tel. (01) 679-7831 or (01) 677-7129.

Dublin Castle is symbolic of English rule over Ireland for 600 years, from the early 13th century until the independence of Ireland in 1922. As such, it is not exactly well liked by many Dubliners.

However, it *is* a great place to visit. There is a guided tour around the grounds and through the **State Apartments**, which formerly served as the residences for the English Viceroys. These elaborate rooms are adorned with rich Donegal carpets and Waterford crystal chandeliers, and are truly luxurious. Today the State Apartments are used primarily for ceremonial affairs from time to time. The remainder of the castle has been converted into government offices.

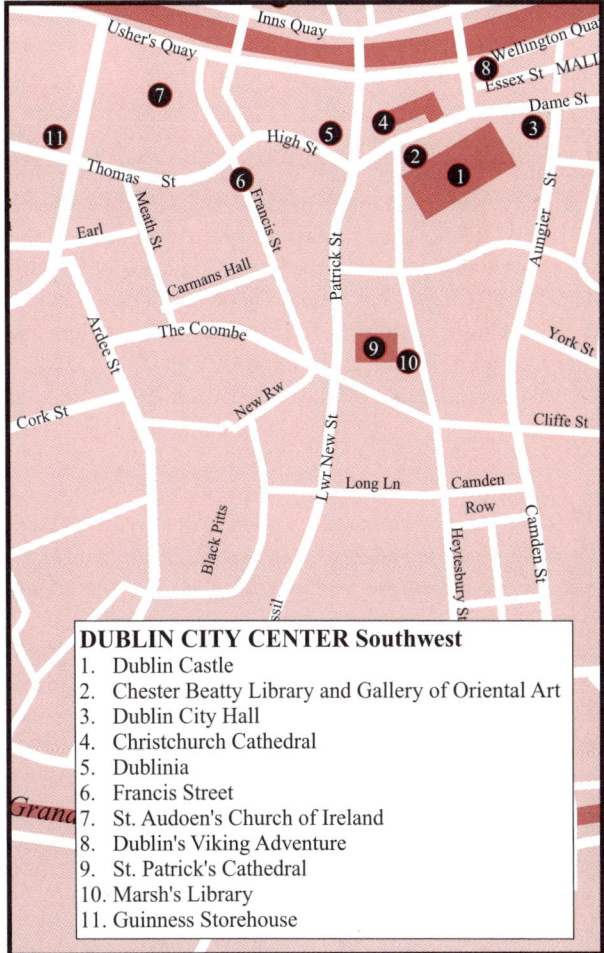

DUBLIN CITY CENTER Southwest

1. Dublin Castle
2. Chester Beatty Library and Gallery of Oriental Art
3. Dublin City Hall
4. Christchurch Cathedral
5. Dublinia
6. Francis Street
7. St. Audoen's Church of Ireland
8. Dublin's Viking Adventure
9. St. Patrick's Cathedral
10. Marsh's Library
11. Guinness Storehouse

Several of the rooms are exceptionally exquisite, particularly the Apollo Room (sometimes called the Music Room), the Round Drawing Room, and the Wedgwood Room. For me, the highlight of the Castle is St. Patrick's Hall. This large room (82 feet by 40 feet) is graced with a hand-painted ceiling and beautiful gilded pillars. It is the venue for Irish presidential inaugurations and various state functions.

The oldest section of Dublin Castle is the Record Tower (the public is not allowed in), a part of the original structure dating back to 1220. Over the years the Record Tower was also called at one time or another the Black Tower, Gunner's Tower, and Wardrobe Tower.

On the grounds of Dublin Castle is the Royal Chapel, also known as the Church of the Holy Trinity. This charming little (little by cathedral standards) church has beautiful oak panels and lovely stained-glass windows. The exterior is embellished with the carved heads of all the kings and queens of England. The Royal Chapel was completed in 1814 based on the designs of Francis Johnston. It served the Anglican Church for over 125 years. However, beginning in 1943, the Catholic Church began using it for their services, and continues to do so today.

2. The Chester Beatty Library and Gallery of Oriental Art
The Clocktower Building behind Dublin Castle is open Monday through Friday from 10am to 5pm, Saturday from 11am to 5pm and Sunday from 1pm to 5pm (closed on Mondays October through April). Admission is free. Tel. (01) 407-0750.

In 1956, Sir Alfred Chester Beatty bequeathed his private collection of Oriental art to Ireland. This outstanding collection of art and antiquities contains over 22,000 items, including rare books and manuscripts, miniature paintings, over 270 ancient copies of the Koran, clay tablets from Babylon, and some of the earliest known Biblical papyri in existence. In fact, their extensive Biblical collection includes Armenian, Coptic, Ethiopian and Syriac texts.

3. Dublin City Hall
Castle Street/Cork Hill, open Monday through Friday 9am to 5pm. Admission is free. Tel. (01) 679-6111.

City Hall is the home of the Dublin Corporation, the Dublin City government. The building was completed in 1769. The entry hall contains fluted columns that tend to cause your eyes to lift upward, where you'll see an impressive domed ceiling. Further on in the Muniment Room you'll find the Dublin City sword and mace. There are no public tours, but you can walk about in the public areas.

4. Christchurch Cathedral

Christchurch Place, open Monday through Friday 9:45am until 5pm and Saturdays and Sundays from 10am to 5pm. Admission is €5 for adults, €2.50 for seniors and children. Access to the crypt is an additional €3 for adults, €1.50 for seniors and children. Tel. (01) 677-8099.

Christchurch Cathedral was built in 1038 for the Norse King Sitric Silkenbeard. Originally a wooden structure, major renovation was undertaken between 1173 and 1220, and the wooden structure was replaced with stonework. In 1831, the cathedral received one final major facelift, and was redone in the Gothic style you see today.

This magnificent cathedral includes a self-guided tour through the ancient crypt below the cathedral. The crypt used to house two very surprising sights, but they have now been moved to the right front of the chapel. There you will find the mummified bodies of a cat and rat that apparently participated in a deadly game of "cat and mouse" in days gone by. The rat raced into an organ pipe with the cat hot on his tail. The cat became lodged in the pipe, and both diner and dinner perished.

The tomb of Strongbow, the first Norman conqueror of Ireland, is located in the cathedral. Not to burst your enthusiastic bubble at seeing the image of the eight-centuries-old great Norman conqueror of Ireland, but Strongbow's actual tomb was destroyed 400 years ago when part of the roof caved in. The tomb was replaced with the effigy of a long-forgotten knight. However, the heart (yes, the actual heart) of St. Lawrence O'Toole is preserved in a metal casket at the east end of the cathedral. He was the Archbishop of Dublin at the time of Strongbow's invasion.

The most noticeable aspects of the interior of Christchurch Cathedral are the elaborate stonework and elegant stained glass that grace the walls of the cathedral. Like St. Patrick's, Christchurch Cathedral belongs to the Church of Ireland.

5. Dublinia

Christchurch Place, open daily from 10am until 5pm from April through September, and Monday through Saturday 11am to 4pm, Sundays and holidays from 10am to 4:30pm. Admission is €5.75 for adults, and €4.50 for students and senior citizens. There is a family pass available (2 adults and 2 children) for €15 (children under 5 are free). Tel. (01) 679-4611.

Located in the Synod Hall across from Christchurch Cathedral, Dublinia (also known as the Dublin Medieval Heritage Centre) allows visitors to step back into 400 years of Dublin history. Dublinia is well worth the visit. You'll receive an audio headset that will guide you through the exhibit, beginning with the invasion of Strongbow in 1170, after which you'll be whisked through the sights and sounds of medieval Dublin up until the mid-1500s. Life-size models and rebuilt city scenes will help transport you back to days gone by. The tour is enlightening, educational, and entertaining – truly an enjoyable way to learn about Ireland's medieval times.

6. Francis Street

This street is the de-facto antique section of Dublin. Although you'll find antique shops elsewhere in Dublin, nowhere is there the concentration as thick as you'll find here on Francis Street, just a block west of St. Patrick's Cathedral. Visitors will be enticed by many of the small shops, some of whose owners are as precious and delightful as the antiques they peddle.

7. Church of Ireland St. Audoen's

High Street, open June through September daily from 9:30am until 5:30pm. Admission is €2 for adults, €1.25 for seniors and students, €1 for children and a family ticket is available for €5.50. Tel. (01) 677-0088.

St. Audoen's Church is the only existing medieval church in Dublin. It was originally called St. Ouen's, but has been altered through the years to its present name. The church is in a lovely park-like setting, surrounded by portions of the old city wall, and includes the only surviving gate to the city, St. Audoen's Arch. The church boasts a set of bells that were made in 1423, and they are thought to be among Ireland's oldest. An extra treat is a good audiovisual presentation called *The Flame on the Hill*, which covers the history of Ireland before the arrival of the Vikings.

If you walk down the steps from the grounds of St. Audoen's to the Arch, you'll be on Cork Street, originally the location of most of Dublin's coffin-makers. Don't mistake this St. Audoen's for the nearby Catholic St. Audoen's. This one is a mere 700 or so years newer than the Catholic church of the same name.

8. Dublin's Viking Adventure

Essex Quay, open Tuesday through Saturday from 10am until 4:30pm. Open Sunday and Monday from 11am to 4:30pm (closed 1pm to 2pm November through February). Admission is €6 for adults, €5 for students and seniors, €4 for children. A family ticket is available for €18. Tel. 679-6040.

Dublin's Viking Adventure does its best to transport its visitors back to the days when Vikings ruled this part of Ireland. You are escorted about the recreated Viking city, including houses and shops and other typical sights – even the sounds and smells. If you can, stay into the evening and enjoy a Viking dinner banquet.

The adventure all takes place within the walls of the converted Saints Michael and John Church. This former Catholic church has also served as a playhouse, so the Viking actors are right at home there. If you're with the kids, this is a good bet.

9. St. Patrick's Cathedral

Patrick Street, open Monday through Friday 9am to 6pm, Saturdays 9am to 5pm, and Sundays 9am to 3pm. Admission is €5 for adults, €4 for students, seniors and children. A family ticket is available for €12. Tel. (01) 475-4817.

If you see only two cathedrals in Dublin, this should be one of them. Aside from the peaceful grounds, the immense beauty of the cathedral is truly a sight to behold. Considered the National Cathedral of the Church of Ireland, St. Patrick's was founded in 1191. But its history goes back much farther. Local historians will tell you that this is perhaps the oldest Christian site in Dublin. It was on this spot that tradition says St. Patrick himself performed baptisms. Originally built outside the Dublin city walls, the location earned St. Patrick's the reputation of being the "church of the people," while Christchurch, which was built within the city walls, was considered by some to be the "church of the government."

Physically, St. Patrick's is impressive. The largest church in Ireland, its west clock tower rises 141 feet above Patrick Street, and the spire atop the tower rises another 101 feet, making the tip of the spire nearly 250 feet above your head. As you walk into St. Patrick's, if it feels like the front of the cathedral is about a football field's length away, you're exactly right: the interior of the cathedral is 300 feet long. As you might expect, St. Patrick's also boasts a number of **stunning stained glass windows**.

It's hard to believe that Oliver Cromwell showed his contempt for this magnificent structure by demanding that his horses be stabled inside the cathedral. This was a practice he replicated throughout the country at other churches, cathedrals, and town halls.

Jonathan Swift, the author of *Gulliver's Travels*, was Dean of St. Patrick's for over 30 years, from 1713 to 1745. His pulpit is still on display in the cathedral, along with sundry items belonging to him. At the west end of the nave you'll find Swift's bust, along with his pointed epitaph which he wrote: "Here he lies, where bitter indignation can no longer lacerate his heart. Go traveler and imitate if you can one who was, to the best of his powers, a defender of Liberty."

The **organ**, one of the more modern additions to the Cathedral, was installed in 1902, and is considered the most robust and powerful in all of Ireland.

The year Columbus set sail for America, two of Ireland's most powerful men, the Earl of Kildare and the Earl of Ormond, had been warring. The Earl of Ormond sought sanctuary in the Chapter House, and a standoff ensued. Tired of the war, the Earl of Kildare approached the Chapter House and chopped a hole in the door. As an act of reconciliation, he thrust his arm through the hole and grasped the hand of his enemy, ending the war. The door – called the "Door of Reconciliation" – is on display in the northeast section of the cathedral.

10. Marsh's Library

St. Patrick's Close, Patrick Street, open Monday from 10am to 1pm, and Wednesday through Friday from 10:30am to 1pm and from 2pm to 5pm, and Saturdays from 10:30am until 1pm. Admission is €2.50 for adults and €1.25 for seniors and children. Tel. (01) 454-3511.

If you are a book lover, this is a place you'll want to visit. Narcissus Marsh, the Archbishop of Dublin, established this as the first public library in Ireland in 1701. The brick exterior of the library is unpretentious, and doesn't prepare you for what you'll find inside. The decor is magnificent; dark oak bookcases and wire cages house over 25,000 books and some 300 rare manuscripts. Most of the books are from the 16th through 18th centuries. Famed writers like Jonathan Swift and James Joyce used the library in their day. The **Stillfleet Collection** alone has over 10,000 books that date back to 1705. Books can no longer be checked out at Marsh's, but you can view some of the volumes in one of the wire cages. Marsh's Library is located behind St. Patrick's Cathedral.

11. Guinness Storehouse

Crane Street, open daily from 9:30am until 5pm. Admission is €14 for adults, €9.50 for students and senior citizens and €5 for children. A family ticket is available for €30. Tel. (01) 453-8364 (information line) or (01) 408-4800 (for reservations for large groups, or to talk to the Hop Store).

A trip to Ireland is not complete unless you try their world famous Guinness beer. And there is no better place than the sprawling, 60-acre Guinness Brewery, where Dubliners swear the beer tastes better! For the uninitiated, Guinness is a dark, heavy, bitter beer with a creamy head served at room temperature. For many, it is an acquired taste, but all beer lovers should try it at least once.

Arthur Guinness founded the brewery on the banks of the River Liffey in 1759, and his descendants have carried on his work. The brewery produces an amazing four million pints of Guinness beer *per day*. Tours of the brewery itself are no longer conducted, but a fine audiovisual presentation on the history of the brewery is available in the Hop Store. At the close of the presentation, a complimentary sample of Guinness is available to those who wish to sample the dark brew. The four-story **Hop Store** has been converted into a museum, and the top floor serves as a venue for art shows.

South of the Liffey – Grafton Street District

12. Molly Malone Statue
Suffolk and Grafton Streets.

O'Connell Street may have had *The Floozie in the Jacuzzi* (it is no longer there), but Grafton Street has the bronze statue of Molly Malone, *The Dish with the Fish!* Molly Malone, standing at the corner of Suffolk and Grafton streets, is a featured character in an old Irish folk song. The song is taught to school children, sung in pubs, and bellowed at rugby, soccer, hurling, and Gaelic football games. The bodice on Molly's dress is so scandalously low (even for a statue!) that she has another name: *The Tart with the Cart.*

13. Trinity College & Book of Kells
College Street, open daily from 8am to 10pm. Admission is free. Tel. (01) 608-2320.

Stately Trinity College is always alive with activity, both inside and outside its grounds. Personally, one of the things we like best about Trinity College is its *presence*. During your stay in Dublin, you will see it in paintings and drawings that are hundreds of years old – it was such an important site in the 16th through 19th centuries. It still is, for that matter.

Trinity College was built during the reign of Queen Elizabeth I in 1592 on the grounds of confiscated Catholic property, the Augustinian Priory of All Hallows. Most of the buildings now date from the early 1700s to the mid-1800s. Its buildings and grounds cover 47 acres in the heart of the city center.

Currently, Trinity College has between 15,000 and 16,000 full-time students. It was the first European university to allow women to earn degrees. However, for most of Trinity College's history, Catholics were barred from entering. Now, you might suppose that is very narrow-minded of Trinity College – but you would be wrong – the ban was by the Catholic Church, not the school! In the 1960s, this ban was lifted and Trinity College has become the renowned university it is today.

Statues of two of Trinity's most famous alumni — orator Edmund Burke and poet Oliver Goldsmith flank the front gate (known creatively as *The Front Gate*). As you move beyond its huge wooden doors, check out the many announcement boards to see what's going on. Often, lunchtime concerts are scheduled, and everyone is welcome to attend.

Without a doubt, the most important holding at Trinity College is the Book of Kells, located in the Trinity College Colonnades. The ornately illustrated four Gospels were written by the monks of the Kells monastery in County Meath. Written (drawn?) in the 9th century, the Book of Kells is four volumes of elaborate ornamental drawings of the four Gospels. The title pages of each Gospel are particularly elaborate.

There are also gorgeous pictures depicting many scenes from Christ's life, including his temptation and arrest.

The Book of Kells is kept in a glass case in a room with muted lighting. Two Gospels are shown at a time, and the pages are turned each day. The pages are calfskin made from 185 calves! As you look at the incredible craftsmanship and stunning artwork of the books, it's hard to imagine that these lovely works were once hidden under a roll of sod to protect them from the ravages of invaders!

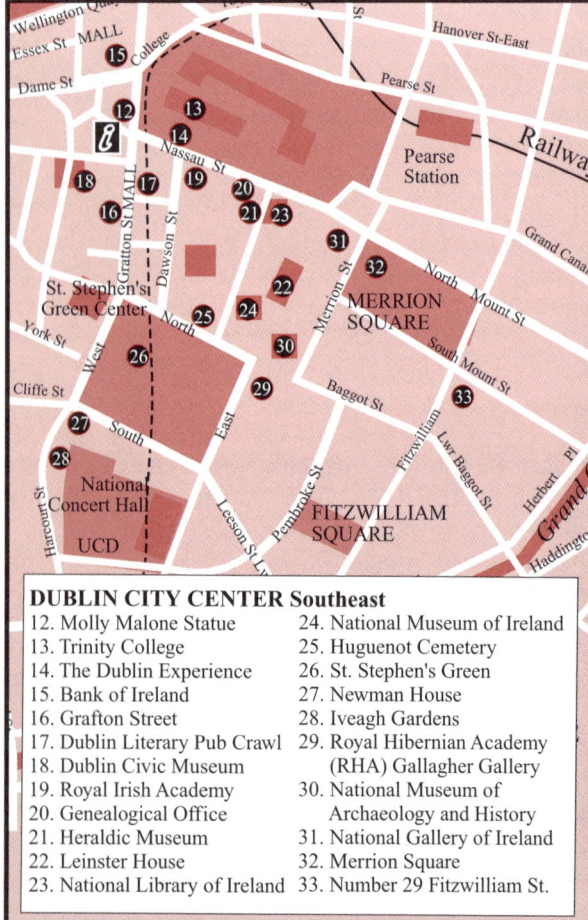

DUBLIN CITY CENTER Southeast

12. Molly Malone Statue	24. National Museum of Ireland
13. Trinity College	25. Huguenot Cemetery
14. The Dublin Experience	26. St. Stephen's Green
15. Bank of Ireland	27. Newman House
16. Grafton Street	28. Iveagh Gardens
17. Dublin Literary Pub Crawl	29. Royal Hibernian Academy
18. Dublin Civic Museum	(RHA) Gallagher Gallery
19. Royal Irish Academy	30. National Museum of
20. Genealogical Office	Archaeology and History
21. Heraldic Museum	31. National Gallery of Ireland
22. Leinster House	32. Merrion Square
23. National Library of Ireland	33. Number 29 Fitzwilliam St.

As you enter the room, there are also cases along the walls (which you walk past while in line) that contain other ancient books, including the **Book of Durrow**, which was written in 675, and is the earliest surviving decorated book of the Gospels. The **Book of Armagh** is another you'll see, and it was written in 807.

To see the Book of Kells, you'll probably have to stand in line, especially during the peak tourist season. But the line moves quickly thanks to college employees who gently encourage you to look and move along your way, a fact you appreciate more when the line moves than you do when you are finally the one who gets to look at the beautiful pages!

Book of Kells info: open Monday through Saturday 9:30am to 5pm, Sunday October through April from noon to 4:30pm. From May to September Sunday hours are 9:30am to 4:30pm (last tour begins half an hour before closing). Admission is €8 for adults, €7 for senior citizens, students and children (children under 12 are free), and there is a family ticket available for €16 (two adults and four children).

After you view of the Book of Kells, you are treated to a fascinating stroll through the lavish **Long Room of the Old Library** on your way out. This impressive room is over 200 feet long and 40 feet wide. For nearly 200 years, Trinity College has been receiving a copy of every book published in Ireland and England, and many of them are on display here in the Old Library. You'll also be in the midst of another of the library's prized possessions: tall oak bookcases filled with over 200,000 old volumes of books. You walk between busts of Homer, Plato, Cicero, Newton, Demosthenes, and many other scholars.

Included in the holdings of the library are first editions of some of Shakespeare's works, as well as copies of the original printing of the *Proclamation of 1916* (Ireland's equivalent of the Declaration of Independence). Watch for a copy of the *Proclamation of 1916* as soon as you enter the Long Hall. (It's usually displayed on your left.) In addition, there is a wonderful 15th-century harp on display. It is in remarkable condition, from its oak and willow woodwork to its 29 brass strings. Legend has it that the harp once belonged to the Irish warrior/poet/king Brian Boru; however, scholars point out that Brian was born some 500 years before the harp was made (spoilsports!).

14. The Dublin Experience
Trinity College Davis Theater, Arts Building, open daily between 10am and 5pm from May through the early October. The shows run every hour on the hour. Admission is €3 for adults (€5 for the combined Book of Kells and the Dublin Experience), €2.50 for students and senior citizens (€4 combined ticket), €1.50 children. Tel. (01) 702-1688.

Trinity College has developed an excellent multimedia presentation on the first thousand years of Dublin history, although it covers much of the same ground other similar presentations in the city do. If you've seen any of them, pass on this one.

15. Bank of Ireland
College Green, open Monday through Friday from 10am to 12:30pm and 1:30pm to 4:00pm. Admission is €1.50. Tel. (01) 671-1671.

Across from Trinity College at the corner of College and Dame Streets is the semi-circular Bank of Ireland. When the edifice was completed in 1729, it housed both houses of Parliament – the House of Commons and the House of Lords, and was the first building ever built for the express purpose of housing Parliament.

In the House of Lords hangs two very old and very impressive tapestries: one portrays William of Orange's defeat of King James II at the Battle of the Boyne in 1690, and the other depicts the 15-week Siege of Derry in 1689. These were significant turning points in Ireland's history. Both tapestries have hung here since 1735, over 250 years! Encased in glass at one end of the room is the ornate speaker's mace.

In 1800, the Irish Parliament did something no other Parliament had done or has since done – they voted themselves out of existence, handing over all governance to the good graces of London. The building was then sold to the Bank of Ireland, who has been its only tenant since then. When the Bank of Ireland purchased the building, they converted the House of Commons into a spacious lobby, but left the House of Lords intact. You can browse around the House of Lords (it's not very big), and nearby attendants will answer questions and tell you a little of the history of the room and building.

16. Grafton Street

Across from Trinity College is Grafton Street, a long pedestrian open-air mall. Grafton Street is a fascinating blend of antique, jewelry, and upscale shops, with a generous mix of *buskers*, street entertainers, ranging from musicians to magicians, jugglers to marionette masters, and a host of other talented individuals. Street peddlers also hawk their wares, ranging from silk ties and silver rings to cassettes and macramé.

To say that Grafton Street is an experience not to be missed would be an understatement. Give yourself plenty of time to stroll along the crowded sidewalks and sample a wee bit of this aspect of Irish culture. The naturally demonstrative nature of the buskers comes through delightfully as they sense an audience gathering around them. Watch for Rocky Thompson, my favorite busker, on Grafton Street sitting astride a small box and playing an old guitar retrofitted with half a dozen piano-like keys, and decorated with various Irish coins glued to the guitar's face. You'll be mesmerized as you listen to Rocky croon out a diverse assortment of tunes, from Irish ballads to Beatles and Bob Dylan songs, to a host of other artists. His unique voice, style and showmanship routinely win him large audiences, not to mention an enviable collection of euro coins and notes.

17. Dublin Literary Pub Crawl

The Literary Pub Crawl meets at The Duke Pub, Duke Street, April 1 through November 27 nightly at 7:30 pm, and Sundays at noon. The rest of the year, they meet Thursday, Friday and Saturday at 7:30 pm, and Sunday at noon. Admission is €11 for adults and €9 for students and children. Tel. (01) 670-5602; E-mail: info@dublinpubcrawl.com.

As you walk south on Grafton Street from Trinity College, look for their tourism-green sign along the left side of the walk directing you onto Duke Street. The **Duke Pub** is about a half block down on your left. The admission charge doesn't cover the cost of any drinks you consume as you move from pub to pub.

Local actors (eight of them) take turns entertaining, informing, shocking, and delighting their guests with tales of Ireland's most noteworthy writers: **Behan**, **Joyce**, **Yeats**, **Wilde**, **Goldsmith**, **Shaw**, and others. Each session is conducted by a two-some (mine were Derrick and Donough). Four or five pubs are part of the tour, as are the grounds of Trinity College. Along the way they regale you with stories and anecdotes from the lives of these writers. You'll find out which journalist referred to himself as a "bicycle built for two" (and why) and learn which writer characterized himself as "A good drinker who had trouble with writing." A rollicking good time, full of literary one-liners, a little irreverence, lots of laughs (a little bawdy at times), and plenty of good, mostly clean fun.

18. Dublin Civic Museum
58 South William Street, open Tuesday through Saturday 10am to 6pm, Sundays 11am to 2pm. Free admission. Tel. (01) 679-4260.

This small museum is a winner for history buffs. The museum's primary focus is the history of Dublin, its people, and its environs. The eclectic collection includes Stone Age implements to Viking tokens to the sculpted head of Admiral Horatio Nelson. Admiral Nelson's image once had a slightly more lofty and dignified position atop Nelson's Pillar beside the General Post Office. However, in 1966 on the fiftieth anniversary of the Easter Rising, Admiral Nelson lost his head, and pillar, to a bomb. Seems as though Irish loyalists resented the good Admiral's image presiding over the goings-on at the GPO!

19. The Royal Irish Academy
19 Dawson Street, open Monday through Friday 10:30am to 5pm. Admission is free. Tel. (01) 676-2570.

The Royal Irish Academy was founded in 1752 and has been located here since 1852. The leading scholarly society in Dublin, the Royal Irish Academy takes great pride in its collection of ancient manuscripts. One of its most valuable is the Psalter of Saint Columcille, a partial copy of the Vulgate version of Psalms. Another is the *Book of the Dun Cow*, a 12th-century manuscript penned at Clonmacnoise. Each week the Academy presents an exhibition of an ancient manuscript.

20. Genealogical Office
2 Kildare Street, open Monday through Friday from 9:30am to 5:30pm. Admission is free.

So your mother was an O'Kelly and your grandfather a Murphy, and you'd like to do a little genealogical research into the family tree? The Genealogical Office is a good place to begin. The employees here are helpful in assisting you to identify and locate those long-lost cousins.

Researching your genealogy in Ireland is like doing it anywhere in the world: the more information you have the better, and the more successful your search is likely to be. Pump Mom and Dad, your grandparents and anyone else in your family for as much information as you can: dates of birth (even an approximate year), county, town, parish, maiden names, parent's names, etc.

21. Heraldic Museum
2 Kildare Street, open Monday through Wednesday from 10am to 8:30pm, Thursday and Friday from 10am to 4:30pm and Saturday from 10am to 12:30pm. Admission is free. Tel. (01) 603-0311.

Co-located with the Genealogical Office, the Heraldic Museum has a fine display of coats of arms that extend back many centuries. Go in and see if you can find yours! In addition, they'll have maps that list the traditional ancestral homes of thousands of Irish surnames. In addition to being a phenomenal resource for genealogical research, the Genealogical office/Heraldic Museum serves as a small museum, with over 500 ancient Irish artifacts on display.

22. Leinster House
Kildare Street, open when Parliament is not in session. Admission is free. Tel. (01) 678-9911.

Built over 250 years ago (1725) for the Duke of Leinster, Leinster House serves as the meeting place for the Irish House of Representatives (*Dail Eireann*) and the Senate (*Seanad Eireann*). Visitors are only admitted to the visitor's gallery upon invitation of a member of Parliament. Check with the Dublin Tourism Center, *Tel. (01) 605-7777,* to see if they can arrange a visit (they often can). The Irish sometimes view their elected officials with humor. As an example, Leinster House has sometimes been referred to as "The National Home for the Terminally Bewildered."

23. The National Library of Ireland
Kildare Street, open Monday through Wednesday from 10am until 9pm, Thursday and Friday 10am until 5pm, and Saturdays 10am until 1:00pm. Admission is free. Tel. (01) 661-8811.

The National Library of Ireland is so much more than a library. First of all, it is a visual treasure. Architecturally stunning, the highlights of the library are the large rotunda and the domed reading room. In addition, exhibits are frequently available on Irish art and history. Many **first editions** are owned by the library, including the works of Ireland's most famous (writing) sons: James Joyce, George Bernard Shaw, Oscar Wilde, etc.

24. National Museum of Ireland
Kildare Street, open Tuesday through Saturday 10am to 5pm and Sunday from 2pm to 5pm. Admission is free (except for special exhibits). Tel. (01) 677-7444.

Located next to the Leinster House on Kildare Street, the National Museum of Ireland was originally the combination of several historical collections. It has a number of fascinating displays which take you through the history of Ireland from the Bronze Age (2200 BC to 700 BC) to the present.

The Treasury Exhibition (the only part of the museum requiring a modest admission fee) includes the lovely Tara Brooch (8th-century), the Ardagh Chalice (8th-century), and the silver and bronzed Cross of Cong (12th-century), and much more. One of the highlights of the museum is a replica of the Newgrange passage grave in County Meath. The actual cross-shaped tomb, about an hour north of Dublin, is nearly 5,000 years old and is wonderfully preserved. If you can't make the drive, be sure and see the replica at the museum. *Ar Thóir na Saoirse*, which means "The Road to Independence," is a permanent exhibit that deals with the major personalities and events that took place from 1916 to 1922 in the struggle for Ireland's independence.

Much like the Smithsonian, there are multiple locations for the National Museum of Ireland. This location contains the archaeology and history exhibits; the location on Merrion Street houses the natural history collection; and the building on Benburb Street houses the decorative arts collection. A shuttle bus runs between the various locations throughout the day.

25. Huguenot Cemetery
St. Stephen's Green North.

As you face the Shelbourne Hotel, about 100 yards to the right of the hotel is the Huguenot Cemetery, final resting place of French Huguenots who left persecution in their native lands for Ireland. Alas, you cannot walk through the grounds, but you can view them from the wrought-iron gates. The sight of the well-maintained cemetery is one of quiet and peaceful tranquility, something the Huguenots found little of during their stressful lives.

26. St. Stephen's Green
At the south end of Grafton Street.

A very peaceful, serene city park. In the 17th century this 22-acre area was an open common, but in the early 1800s it became a private garden for residents whose property circled it. An annual one guinea (about $1.75) maintenance fee was charged for upkeep and access to the gardens. In 1877, Sir Arthur Guinness (of brewery fame) was instrumental in passing an act of Parliament that opened the park to the public. Because of his magnanimous gesture, Dubliners allowed him to personally pay for many of the improvements to the park, including the lake, fountains, trees and many of the gardens.

There are a number of memorials in the park that are worthy of your attention. The Romanesque arch over the main entrance at the northwest corner of the park is called the Fusiliers Arch, and it is a memorial to the Dublin Fusiliers who fought and died during the Boer War. There is a memorial dedicated to the memory of W. B. Yeats. Don't miss the fountain and statue of the Three Fates, a statue given to the Irish by a grateful German government for the relief they provided to the needy at the close of World War II. Other individuals memorialized in St. Stephen's Green include James Joyce, Wolfe Tone, and those who perished in the potato famine.

There is a children's playground, lots of ducks for the children and you to feed, a Victorian bandstand (where free lunchtime concerts are given throughout the summer), and a unique garden designed especially for the blind. The plants are labeled in Braille, and they are also resilient enough to be handled.

27. Newman House
85/86 St. Stephen's Green South, open June through August Tuesday through Friday from noon until 5pm, Saturdays 2pm until 5pm. Admission is €5 for adults, and €4 for children and senior citizens. Tel. (01) 706-7422.

Across the street from the south side of St. Stephen's Green is

Newman House. Newman House is named after **Cardinal John Henry Newman**, who founded the first Catholic University in Dublin at Number 86, St. Stephen's Green South. **James Joyce** was one of the more illustrious individuals to call the Catholic University his alma mater (he attended from 1899 to 1902). In fact, one of the rooms has been renovated to look as classroom would have looked at the turn of the century. The period furniture nicely accents the masterful plaster work in both houses. The small admission fee includes a guided tour of both buildings, as well as a short video presentation on the history of the building.

28. Iveagh Gardens
Behind Newman House and Iveagh House. Open Monday through Saturday from 8:00am to sundown and Sunday from 10am to sundown. Admission is free.

The entrance to the gardens is around the corner, left at Harcourt Street, then left on Clonmel Street to the garden gate.

29. Royal Hibernian Academy (RHA) Gallagher Gallery
15 Ely Place, open Monday through Wednesday and Friday through Saturday from 11am to 5pm; Thursday from 11am to 9pm, Sundays from 2pm until 5pm. Admission is free. Tel. (01) 661-2558.

This small Gallery houses an eclectic collection of Irish and continental art. With several other more notable art museums close by, this one tends to get passed over by most visitors.

30. Natural Museum of Archaeology and History
Merrion Street, open Tuesday through Saturday from 10am to 5pm, Sunday from 2:00pm until 5pm. Admission is free. Tel. (01) 667-7444.

The Natural History Museum, founded in 1857, is part of the National Museum of Ireland. George Bernard Shaw reportedly said that he owed much of his education to the gallery and showed his gratitude by leaving one-third of his estate to the museum.

The collection includes an outstanding exhibit of **Irish fauna**, including an especially impressive skeleton of a giant Irish deer, a distant cousin of the elk, African and Asian animals, and two large whale skeletons suspended from the ceiling. (The whales are former Irish residents *of sorts* - they washed up on Irish shores!) The museum is also internationally renowned for its extensive entomological collection. If you are vacationing with children, I'm sure they'd enjoy this museum.

31. National Gallery of Ireland
Merrion Square West, open Monday through Saturday 9:30am to 5:30pm (Thursday until 8:30pm), Sunday from noon until 5:30pm. Admission is free. Tel. (01) 661-5133.

Established by an Act of Parliament in 1854, the National Gallery of Ireland spent 10 years collecting paintings, sculptures, and other pieces of art before opening in January 1864. The grand opening of the museum boasted over 100 paintings and numerous statues. Today there are over 2,400 paintings, 300 sculptures and an incredible assortment of various other pieces to catch your eye.

If you are hoping to see works of art by Irish painters, you won't be disappointed. I suppose every major Irish artist – and many not-so-major artists – are represented here. In addition, there is a fine **European collection**, including works by such notables as Rembrandt, Degas, El Greco, Goya, Monet, Reynolds, Rubens, Titian, Van Dyck, and others. One of the museum's most extraordinary aspects is a four story circular staircase lined with paintings of three centuries worth of notable personalities in Irish history, a kind of wall of fame.

Guided tours are offered on Saturday afternoons at 3pm and Sundays at 2:30pm, 3:15pm, and 4pm. If you find yourself here around lunchtime, there is an award-winning self-serve restaurant available to meet your gastronomical needs.

32. Merrion Square
Laid out in the center of one of the most impressive displays of Georgian architecture in the city, Merrion Square is a place to get away from the omnipresent Dublin traffic. Merrion

Square is about a half-block south and east of the Trinity College grounds. The park dates from 1762, and is a lovely assemblage of gardens, shrubs, and trees. Over the years, a number of Ireland's most important and esteemed citizens called the fine Georgian townhouses around Merrion Square home, including Oscar Wilde's parents (Number 1), Daniel O'Connell (Number 58), W. B. Yeats (Numbers 52 and 82) and the Duke of Wellington (Number 24 Upper Merrion Street). Many of the homes have plaques identifying their famous inhabitants.

33. Number Twenty-Nine Fitzwilliam Street
Open Tuesday through Saturday from 10am to 5pm, Sunday from 2pm to 5pm. Admission is €3.50 for adults, €1.50 for seniors and students, children under 16 free. Tel. (01) 702-6165.

The National Museum of Ireland and the Electricity Supply Board have combined their talents and funds to restore Number Twenty-Nine as it likely was in the late 18th century – the home of a middle-class family. Great attention to detail has been given to everything from the woodwork to the furnishings, walls and ceilings. Take special note of the floor and window coverings, as well as the numerous paintings. Number Twenty-Nine is a little more subdued than a similar exhibit at the Newman House, but both are nice.

North of the Liffey

O'Connell Street runs north for two blocks from the River Liffey, but it is one of the most important streets in Dublin. Once a grand thoroughfare where the ladies and gentlemen of Dublin's High Society liked to be seen, today it is not quite as impressive , although the city is working hard to revitalize it. The wide central island is punctuated with large green trees and statues of Irish greats (see sidebar on the next page for details about these great Irish leaders).

34. General Post Office (GPO)

O'Connell Street, open Monday through Saturday 8am until 8pm, Sundays from 10:30am to 6:30pm. Tel. (01) 872-8888.

This is probably the most talked-about building in Dublin. It is the main post office, and as such everyone is familiar with it. But its mark on history goes much beyond postal service: it was the flash point of the 1916 Easter Rising. It was from the seized GPO that Irish rebel leaders proclaimed their message of a new republic. The ensuing battle destroyed most of the area around O'Connell Street. Some of the GPO's massive stone columns still bear the scars of flying bullets. As a result of the fighting, the GPO was virtually gutted by fire and British artillery. Its renovation was completed in 1929 and faithfully restored the GPO to its former grandeur. The words of the proclamation read by the rebel leaders on that fateful Easter morning is inscribed in a green marble plaque in the GPO. All those who signed the proclamation also signed their death warrants. All were taken to Kilmainham Prison and executed.

Inside the GPO in a window looking out onto O'Connell Street is a magnificent statue of Cuchulainn (pronounced Koo-hoo'-lin). He was a legendary Irish warrior who has been immortalized by generations of Irish storytellers and idolized by generations of Irish children. He was the leader of the Red Branch Knights, an elite army charged with defending Ulster from her many enemies. As famous and colorful as Davey Crockett, Daniel Boone, and Paul Bunyan, Cuchulainn is a legendary

The Statues of O'Connell Street

Who were the men whose statues you now see on O'Connell Street's central island? Daniel O'Connell was a Dublin mayor and winner of Catholic emancipation). William Smith O'Brien was a leader of one of Ireland's many rebellions against British authority. Sir John Gay was a newspaper editor. James Larkin was a historic union leader. Father Theobald Mathew was a revered priest known as "the apostle of temperance, and honored for his tireless efforts during a cholera epidemic in 1832. Charles Stewart Parnell was a key figure in the Home Rule campaign.

DUBLIN CITY CENTER Northeast

34. General Post Office
35. Spire of Dublin
36. Henry Street
37. Garden of Remembrance
38. Dublin Writer's Museum
39. National Wax Museum
40. Hugh Lane Municipal Gallery of Modern Art
41. St. Mary's Pro-Cathedral
42. The Custom House
49. National Botanic Gardens

Irish hero of epic proportion. While he was probably a real person, his actual exploits are now shrouded in so much myth and hero-worship that it is hard to differentiate between fact and fiction. The annals report that after a lifetime of warring, Cuchulainn fought in one last ferocious battle. Fearlessly facing a daunting number of foes, he bravely and single-handedly fought on and on, spilling the blood of many enemies.

Mortally wounded, he is said to have lashed himself to a stone so that he could face his enemies while remaining on his feet. His foes wouldn't approach his body, the legend says, until a bird landed on the shoulder of the lifeless warrior. The statue depicts his last moments. It is an appropriate tribute to those few warriors who took on the British Empire almost single-handedly and wrested Ireland from her grasp. Out front of the GPO, there are three magnificent stone statues atop the portico representing three other legendary figures: Mercury, Hibernia, Fidelity.

The intersection in front of the GPO – Henry and North Earl streets and O'Connell Street – was formerly the location of one of the city's most recognizable landmarks, the **Nelson Pillar**. A 135-foot pillar, complete with spiral staircase leading to the viewing platform at the top, was a tribute to British Admiral Nelson. On a March night in 1966, a tremendous blast reduced the pillar to rubble, an act of Irish loyalists who resented Admiral Nelson's lofty position in the city center. The demolition took place just prior to the 50th anniversary of the 1916 Easter Rising.

35. Spire of Dublin
The Nelson Pillar has finally been replaced – sort of – with the Spire of Dublin. Another pillar has been erected at the same intersection where Lord Nelson once stood. In 2003, Dublin's city fathers erected a 393-foot pole on the site. Dubliners have given it a number of less inspiring titles, including *The Stiletto in the Ghetto*, *The Spike* and *The Nail in the Pale*. Alas, to make room for the Spire of Dublin, one of Dublin's famous statues was removed: the Anna Livia Millennium Fountain. Anna Livia represented the River Liffey. The stylized woman laying

in the midst of bubbling waters was known by the common appellation *The Floozie in the Jacuzzi*. One can only hope that one day Anna Livia will find her way back into Dublin's sights to see.

36. Henry Street
Bisects O'Connell Street one block north of the River Liffey.

Like Grafton Street on the south of the river, Henry Street is a pedestrian shopping area. Grafton Street has largely replaced it as *the* shopping street in Dublin, but it is still crowded with shoppers most hours of the day and evening. The stores are a little older and the architecture a little more tired, but the atmosphere is similar to Grafton Street.

About a half block off O'Connell Street on the right is a large tile mosaic on the walkway that announces the entrance to **Moore Street**, which for generations has been the fruit, vegetable, and flower market of Dublin. You can hear the (mostly) women vendors shouting to call your attention to their produce. In days gone by, many of the shops lining Moore Street were butcher shops, but discount stores and other shops have slowly replaced them. It's a fun place to go, and it's especially colorful and cheery on a sunny day.

37. Garden of Remembrance
Parnell Square. Open daily from November through February from 11am to 4pm, from 11am to 7pm March and April, from 9:30am to 8pm from May through September, and from 11am to 7pm in October. Admission is free.

On the fiftieth anniversary of the Easter Rising of 1916, which led to Ireland's independence, the Garden of Remembrance was built to commemorate those who gave their lives that Ireland might be a free nation. (Think of it as the Minuteman statue in Lexington, Massachusetts.) This is a very peaceful and contemplative place where visitors can think about Irish patriots who gave their lives for a free Ireland.

The square features an ornamental pond in the form of a crucifix, and the setting is very serene and peaceful. Just beyond the small pond is a statue that looks like children chasing geese and making them fly away. It is in reality a statue of the children of Lir, who were turned into swans (according to legend).

38. Dublin Writer's Museum
18/19 Parnell Square, open September through May Monday through Saturday from 10am to 5pm, and Sundays from 11am to 5pm; from June through August it is open Monday through Friday 10am to 6pm, Saturday from 10am to 5pm, and Sundays from 11am to 5pm. Admission is €6.50 for adults, €5.50 for students and €4 for children. There is a family ticket for €18 (2 adults and 3 or 4 children). Tel. (01) 872-2077.

Ireland has always loved its writers and poets, and there always been a special place for them in the heart of every Irish man and woman. Now there is a museum for them, too. The Dublin Writer's Museum opened in 1991 and has quickly become one of Dublin's top attractions. It is one of the most elegant, tasteful and well thought-out museums in Ireland.

This exquisitely restored Georgian home houses the Gorham Library on the first floor. Be sure to take a look at its beautiful ceiling. Permanent exhibits in the museum feature famed Irish authors such as Samuel Beckett, Brendan Behan, George Bernard Shaw, Jonathan Swift, and Oscar Wilde. Paintings, photographs, letters, and memorabilia are all part of the various exhibits.

Adjacent to the museum is the Irish Writer's Centre, a gathering place for current writers to meet, talk, and host readings. If the exhibits spark an interest in the works of these writers, there is a bookstore that sells most of the works of the authors represented in the museum. If it's food you're thinking of, they also have a cafe on-site.

39. National Wax Museum
Granby Row, open Monday through Saturday from 10am to 5pm, and Sunday from noon to 5pm. Admission is €6 for adults, senior citizens and students €5, children €3.50. A family ticket is available for €16.50. Tel. (01) 872-6340.

It's okay for a wax museum, but to be honest, we find most wax museums, well, sort of lifeless. You can see the Pope, along with Madonna's paraffin persona here, along with a host of Irish personalities.

40. Hugh Lane Municipal Gallery of Modern Art
Parnell Square, open Tuesday through Thursday from 9:30am to 6pm, Friday and Saturday from 9:30am to 5pm and Sunday from 11am to 5pm. Admission is free, although special exhibits do cost a slight fee. Tel. (01) 874-1903.

Built in the mid-18th century, this former townhouse of Lord Charlemont has been restored and now houses a fine collection of modern art. Works by Picasso, Monet, Renoir, Degas, and Manet are all part of the collection of artworks owned at one time by Hugh Lane. Upon Mr. Lane's death on the *Lusitania* off the southwest coast of Ireland in 1915 (which some claim was the work of the English to bring America into the first world war, but that's another story), his collection of art was to go to the Dublin Corporation.

But several years prior to his death, Mr. Lane was angered when the Dublin Corporation decided not to build a special gallery to house his collection, so he stipulated that 39 of his paintings were to go to London instead. However, after his death, a contested (unwitnessed) codicil was discovered reversing his decision and bequeathing the paintings to the Dublin Corporation, his original preference. The collection was tied up in legal proceedings for nearly 50 years until London and Dublin decided on a compromise: the paintings would rotate every five years between the two cities. Included with Lane's collection are a number of other fine works by 19th and 20th-century artists, as well as a room devoted to stained glass artisan Harry Clarke.

41. St. Mary's Pro-Cathedral
Marlborough Street, open Monday through Saturday from 8am to 6:30pm, Sunday 8am to 7pm. Admission is free. Tel. (01) 874-5441.

Six columns support a massive portico at the front of St. Mary's

Pro-Cathedral. If you've been to the Temple of Theseus in Athens, those six columns might make you think that the architect was trying to imitate it, and you'd be right. It was indeed patterned after the Athenian temple. Completed in 1825, the interior is done in Grecian-Doric architectural style, and seems a little out of place in the capitol city of the Emerald Isle.

This church (it was never endowed with cathedral status) has been the location of the funerals for key government officials for years. It is considered the main Catholic church in Ireland. The crypt is open irregular times, but is an interesting place to explore. Ask if it is open when you arrive, or call ahead for times when you can visit it.

42. The Custom House
Custom House Quay. Visitor Center open mid-March through November on Monday through Friday from 10am to 12:30 pm, and November through mid-March Wednesday through Friday from 10am to 12:30pm, and Sunday from 2pm to 5pm. Admission is €1, with a family ticket available for €3.

If you spend any time whatsoever in Dublin, you are certain to wonder what the large, obviously governmental-type building is that faces the River Liffey two blocks east of O'Connell Street. It is the Custom House, and it is a very impressive sight, especially at night when it is brightly lit.

The Custom House is a building that evokes strong feelings of pride in Dubliners – it really is a beautiful, stately building.

But that wasn't always the case. When construction began in 1781, opponents hired ruffians on more than one occasion to attack the builders. Notwithstanding these efforts and numerous death threats to the builder, James Gandon, work on the building continued – but he felt the threats were serious enough that he began wearing his sword to the job site.

A suspicious fire broke out in a portion of the unfinished building in 1789, but the damage was repaired and the Custom House opened on schedule in 1791. But, unlike characters in fairy tales, the Custom House did not live happily ever after. Another fire struck in 1833, and then a fire of monumental proportions devastated the structure in 1921. Local fire crews were unsuccessful in putting out the fire, and it burned out of control for five days. The fire was so hot that it melted brass door fittings and cracked stonework.

Once again restoration and repair work put the building back in commission. In the early 1970s, it was determined that additional cracks in the stonework, probably caused by the fire in 1921, would need to be fixed. An aggressive restoration program was completed in the early 1990s. The Custom House has once again been restored to its prior grandeur. And you benefit from the work.

43. Four Courts
Inns Quay, open Monday through Friday 10am to 4pm. Admission is free. Tel. (01) 872-5555.

The Four Courts is a landmark building. Its dome, sitting majestically above the River Liffey is a familiar site, and very impressive at night. Housing the Irish Law Courts, the Four Courts has been on the Dublin scene since its completion in 1802.

During the Irish Civil War in 1922, the Four Courts was nearly destroyed by fire and artillery shelling and the Public Records Office next to it was destroyed, along with generations of irreplaceable legal, land, and genealogical records, a most regrettable loss. Fortunately the building was not razed, and years of renovation have restored it to its previous glory.

The front portico is supported by six massive columns, and Moses, the Law Giver, stands tall at the center of the top of the portico and is flanked by the statues of Justice and Mercy. Behind and above the portico is an immense circular dome. If you have the time, be sure and visit the upper rotunda of the dome. It provides some nice views of Dublin.

44. St. Michan's Church

Church Street, open March through October Monday through Friday from 10am to 12:30pm, and from 2pm to 4:30pm, and Saturdays from 10am until 12:45pm, and November through February Monday through Friday 12:30pm to 3:30pm, and Saturday 10am to 12:45pm. Admission to the vaults is €3.50 for adults, and €3 for senior citizens and €2.50 for children. Tel. (01) 872-4154.

Originally built in 1095 as a Viking parish church (the only one north of the River Liffey for over 500 years), St. Michan's was rebuilt to its current state in 1686, and has had several facelifts since then. Most of the renovations have been faithful to the original workmanship of the church. As you peruse the interior, be sure and notice the beautiful woodwork throughout the chapel.

Legend has it that **Handel** played St. Michan's magnificent 18th-century organ while composing *The Messiah*. (It's the Irish equivalent of "George Washington slept here.")

One of the oddities at St. Michan's is the "stool of repentance," where misbehaving parishioners did public penance. Perhaps the most unusual aspect of St. Michan's is the partially mummified remains of three 17th-century people in the vaults. The limestone in the ground of the vaults removed moisture from the air, preserving the bodies remarkably well. If the mummified cat and mouse at Christchurch made you queasy, you might want to pass on these fellows.

West Dublin

45. Phoenix Park

This park originally opened to the public over 250 years ago. It is the largest city park in Europe at over 1,700 acres, and a delightful place to visit. If you enjoy parks and have the time, you could easily spend a half day here; a full day if you also go to the zoo, or watch a polo match or a cricket game. With green fields punctuated by pools and ponds, the park serves as a relaxing contrast to the hustle and bustle of the city. Phoenix Park is about two miles from Dublin's city center.

As you enter the park from its main gate on the southeast side, the 195-foot monument honoring Arthur Wellesley, the first **Duke of Wellington**, greets you. You may ask yourself why this British general who defeated Napoleon at Waterloo rates a monument in Dublin? After all, a similar monument to the British Admiral Nelson – another victor over Napoleon – was so ill-received by Dubliners that it was blown to pieces by some unknown hand. The answer is simple: Wellington was a native Dubliner. Despite his choice of armies, his victory at Waterloo earned him fame and hero status in Ireland. An ironic tidbit of historical trivia is the fact that Arthur Wellesley detested his Irish roots. When queried about his Irish beginnings, he reportedly replied, "The fact that I was born in a stable does not make me a horse." Point well made!

Across the road from Wellington's monument is the **People's Garden**, a lovely set of banked gardens surrounding a small lake. Just ahead on your right is the **Dublin Zoo**, which was founded in 1831. It has a wide variety of animals, and an area for the children to get "up close and personal" with a number of less exotic creatures like rabbits, chickens, and goats.

The **polo grounds** are just beyond the zoo, and practices or matches are fun to watch, whether you understand all the rules or not (I don't). The horses are magnificent, and to see them wheeling and charging is a real treat. The riders aren't bad either.

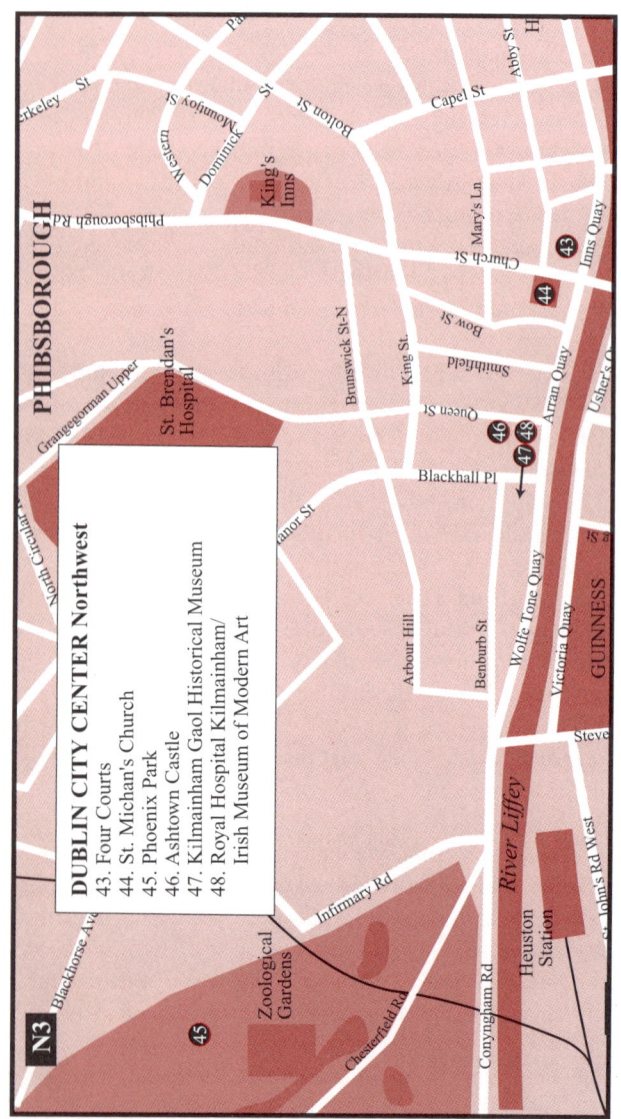

DUBLIN CITY CENTER Northwest
43. Four Courts
44. St. Michan's Church
45. Phoenix Park
46. Ashtown Castle
47. Kilmainham Gaol Historical Museum
48. Royal Hospital Kilmainham/
    Irish Museum of Modern Art

PHIBSBOROUGH

King's Imns

Capel St

Mary's Ln

Church St

Bow St

Brunswick St-N

King St

Smithfield

Queen St

Arran Quay

Usher's Q

Blackhall Pl

Arbour Hill

Benburb St

Wolfe Tone Quay

Victoria Quay

GUINNESS

River Liffey

Infirmary Rd

Heuston Station

Conyngham Rd

Chesterfield Rd

Zoological Gardens

Blackhorse Av

North Circular

Grangegorman Upper

Phibsborough Rd

St. Brendan's Hospital

Dominick

Western

Mountjoy St

Berkeley St

Bolton St

Capel St

Abby St

Imns Quay

Steve

John's Rd West

43
44
46
47 48
45
N3

On the far south side of the park is the former site of the **Dublin Dueling Grounds**, where the gentility of Dublin came to shoot at each other in days gone by. Today the area hosts far more civilized hostility and competition in the form of hurling, cricket and football. Matches/games are typically played around 3:00pm on Saturdays and Sundays from mid-May through September.

The beautiful park is not named after the mythological bird that rises from the ashes, but rather from the Irish words *fionn uisce* (clear water), which sounds like Phoenix in English. On nice days, elderly men and women in their Sunday best sit on many of the park benches enjoying the weather and watching the people go by. Families cavort on the grass, visit the zoo, and feed the omnipresent ducks. Lovers walk arm and arm oblivious to the beauty around them.

The main claim to fame of **Dublin Zoo** is that lions breed here almost as well as they do in the wild. They are one of the few zoos in the world that can make that claim. And they do it in a big way – over 700 lions have been bred here since they began the program in 1851. The famous MGM lion claims the Dublin Zoo as his birthplace. *Located in Phoenix Park; open March through September on Monday through Saturday from 9:30am until 6pm and Sunday from 10:30am to 9pm, October through February on Monday through Saturday from 9:30am until dusk and Sunday from 10:30am to dusk. Admission is €12.50 for adults, €10 for students, €8 for seniors and children under 16, children 3 and younger are free. Family tickets available for €35-44. Tel. (01) 677-1425.*

46. Ashtown Castle
Phoenix Park, open daily from mid-March through May from 9:30am until 5pm, daily from June through September from 10am to 6pm, daily in October from 9:30am to 5pm, November and December on Saturday and Sunday from 9:30am to 4:30pm, and January through mid-March on Saturday and Sunday from 9:30am to 4:30pm. Admission is €2.50 for adults, €1.90 for seniors and students, €1.20 for children and a family ticket is available for €6. Tel. (01) 677-0095.

This unassuming medieval fortress was built in the 17th century. The small visitors center hosts presentations on the history of Phoenix Park and on the various plants and animals you'll find there.

47. Kilmainham Gaol Historical Museum

Inchicore Road, open April through September daily from 9:30am until 5pm, and October through March Monday through Saturday from 9:30am until 5:30pm and Sunday from 10am until 5pm. The last tour begins one hour before closing. Admission is €5 for adults, €3.50 for seniors and €2 for students and children, and a family ticket is available for €11. Tel. (01) 677-6801.

Step into the darker side of Ireland's past. This restored prison gives its guests a peek into the terrible conditions endured by Irish patriots awaiting execution or a one-way ticket to Australia. From its first political prisoners in 1796 until its last in 1924, Kilmainham Gaol meant nothing but misery for Irish patriots. Among the most infamous acts committed here was the execution of those who penned their names to the Proclamation of the Republic in 1916 (the Irish equivalent of the Declaration of Independence).

After the last prisoner was released in 1924 (it happened to be the former president of the rebel Irish Republic, Eamon de Valera) the prison fell into disrepair and seemed destined for the wrecking ball. It was through the efforts of a few who didn't wish for this chapter to be forgotten that the jail was restored. You'll chill as you view the Hanging Room and you'll cringe as you walk about the prison yard where executions took place. A short audiovisual presentation is included in the tour, and gives you the highlights of the Irish struggle for independence.

48. Royal Hospital Kilmainham/Irish Museum of Modern Art

Kilmainham Lane, open Tuesday through Saturday 10am to 5:30pm, Sundays from noon until 5:30pm. Admission is free. Tel. (01) 612-9900.

This splendid building was formerly the Royal Hospital

Kilmainham (RHK). It was built in 1684 after the manner of *Les Invalides* in Paris, and its original purpose was to house ill and infirm soldiers, a tribute to their service to Britain. After the establishment of the Irish Free State in 1922, the building was closed and fell into severe disrepair. A 15-year, $30,000,000 renovation project has paid handsome dividends – the building is once again a grand structure.

Now the RHK is home to the Irish Museum of Modern Art (IMMA): four galleries surrounding a large and lovely courtyard. An eclectic array of 20th-century art is exhibited throughout the museum, and there always seems to be a one-man show, or theme exhibit going on. The Banqueting Hall is now the site of frequent concerts and special activities. Perhaps the prettiest room is the chapel, which has rich wood paneling and a Baroque ceiling. This grand structure is worth a visit even if you have no interest in modern art.

49. National Botanic Gardens

Glasnevin Road, Glasnevin, open during the summer months Monday through Saturday from 9am until 6pm, Sundays from 11am to 6pm; open during the winter months Monday through Saturday from 10am to 4:30pm, and Sundays from 11am to 4:30pm. Admission is €2. Tel. (01) 837-7596 or (01) 837-4388.

This is a real treat and worth the short drive (or bus – numbers 13, 19, or 34, or cab ride). Visitors have enjoyed these gardens for over 200 years.

The gardens boast over 20,000 plant species spread over 45 acres, but the oversized arboretum threatens to steal the show. Completed in 1869, it recently went through an extensive restoration. The greenhouses – over 400 feet of them – house an astounding variety of exotic plants and trees, such as orchids, banana trees, and palm trees. The Tolka River runs through the gardens. Cross over the wooden bridge into the extraordinary rose gardens for a special treat.

The National Botanic Gardens are a little further north than many of the other sites north of the Liffey – it's about a two-mile walk from the Liffey.

Day Trips

If you want to spend some time outside Dublin, there are a number of day trips you can take to experience a little more of Ireland. Listed below are several day trips – two can be easily made in a day, leaving in the morning and returning in the early evening. For one of them, the Southwest Ireland excursion, you will probably want to spend the night at your destination, although you could do it in one long day.

DAY TRIP ONE: NEWGRANGE
Featured sights: Newgrange, Mellifont Abbey, Monasterboice and the Hill of Tara

Newgrange is one of the most ancient and intriguing sites in Ireland (one of our favorites), and it is a short bus or car drive from downtown Dublin. If you only have time for one day trip during your visit to Dublin, this is the one we suggest. Several tour companies offer day trips to Newgrange, but we recommend the one offered by **Bus Eireann**, the Irish national bus line.
- 8am – depart Busaras Store Street Station in Dublin
- 9:45am – arrive Drogheda
- 10:15am – depart Drogheda for Donore
- 10:25am – arrive at Donore

Buses return from Newgrange throughout the day, but here is a schedule that will give you time to tour the visitors' center as well as see Newgrange, and return to Dublin before it gets too late:

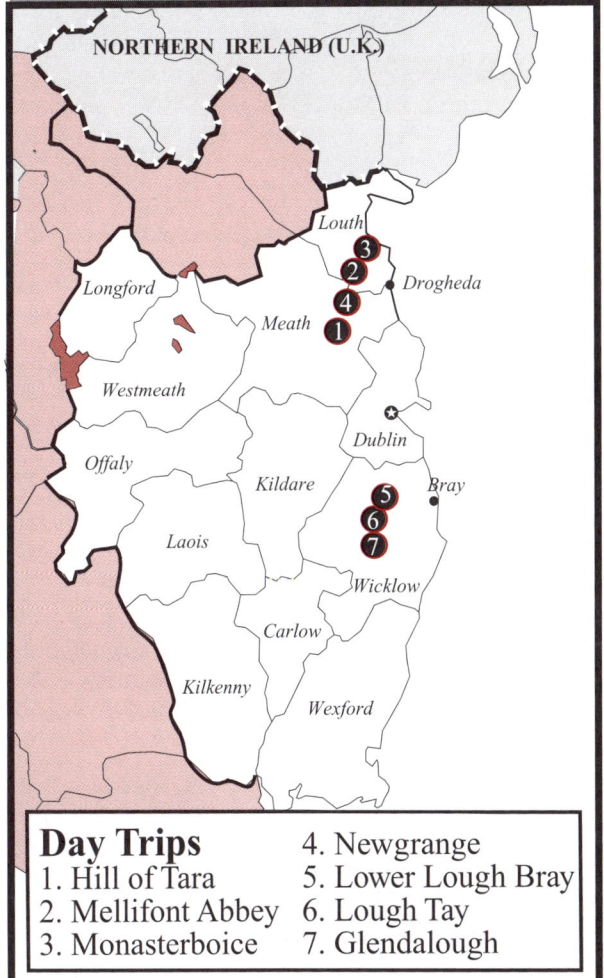

Day Trips
1. Hill of Tara
2. Mellifont Abbey
3. Monasterboice

4. Newgrange
5. Lower Lough Bray
6. Lough Tay
7. Glendalough

- 4:10pm – depart Donore
- 4:20pm – arrive Drogheda
- 5:15pm – depart Drogheda
- 6:30pm – arrive Busaras Store Street Station in Dublin

If you prefer to drive, catch a bus or cab to the Dublin airport and rent a car. From the airport, head north toward Drogheda on either the N1 or the N2. Watch for signs directing you to Newgrange (it is near Slane). Newgrange is between the N1 and the N2.

Newgrange is accessed via a modern new visitors' center about a two-minute walk from where Bus Eireann drops you off in Donore.

Newgrange

Open March through April daily from 10am to 5pm, May daily from 9am to 6:30pm, June through mid-September from 9am to 7pm, mid-September to the end of September daily from 9am to 6:30pm, October daily from 9:30am to 5pm, and November through February daily from 9:30am to 5pm. Admission to the visitor centre only is €2 for adults, €1.50 for seniors and students, €1 for children and a family ticket is available for €5. Admission to the visitor centre and Newgrange is €5 for adults, €3.50 for senior citizens and students, €2.50 for children, and a family ticket is available for €15. Admission to the visitor centre, Newgrange and Knowth is €7 for adults, €5 for senior citizens and students, €3.25 for children, and a family ticket is available for €17.25.

Nestled into the Boyne River Valley in County Meath are a number of important archaeological discoveries made in recent years. Newgrange, Dowth, and Knowth, within close proximity to one another, are the sites of three ancient burial mounds. Of the three, Newgrange's cross-shaped passage grave is the most impressive. Inside Newgrange, visitors will be led down a passage lined with massive stones and into the central burial chamber.

The Newgrange mound is a well-preserved grave dating back to nearly 3,000 BC. During the winter solstice (December 21), rays from the sun glide down the narrow passageway gradually lighting the burial chamber. For those unable to be at Newgrange during the winter solstice, modern technology recreates the effect. At 8:58am on December 21 of each year, the rising sun strikes an aperture in the roof of the passage grave. The sunlight is directed down into the passage grave, and as the sun rises its rays slowly move down the passage until they arrive in the main burial chamber, illuminating it. The rest of the year the effect is simulated by shining a light down the passage and into the burial chamber, as though it was really December 21, simulating the path the sun's rays take.

The burial mounds at Dowth and Knowth are also impressive, though neither has the dramatic winter solstice effect Newgrange offers. Dowth, in fact, has two chambers to its passage-tomb, and Knowth offers two main tombs surrounded by 18 others. Both Dowth and Knowth are in the process of excavation, and sometimes parts of them are open to visitors. When they are, the hours are the same as those listed above for Newgrange.

All three sites offer splendid examples of ancient artistic/ritualistic craftsmanship, as the tombs are all graced with wonderful stone carvings. These are impressive reminders of ancient man's devotion to his god or gods. These were the burial sites of the ancient kings of Ireland, and are well worth a visit.

If you have taken the bus to Newgrange, then your tour will be limited to Newgrange and the visitors' center. If you drove here, however, since you are so close, we suggest that you visit several other renowned Irish sites: Mellifont Abbey, Monasterboice, and the Hill of Tara.

Mellifont Abbey ruins
Very near Newgrange, just off the N51 on the R168 is the town of Tullyallen. Tel. (041) 982-6459. Open from May through October daily from 10am to 6pm. Admission is €1.90 for adults, €1.20 for seniors and €0.70 children; family ticket €5.

Mellifont Abbey was founded in 1142 by St. Malachy O'Morgair, and was the first Cisterian monastery in Ireland. Only bits and pieces of the original buildings are still available to see, but the remains are enough to tell you it was an extensive site in its day. In fact, its Irish name, *An Mhainistir Mhor*, means "The Big Monastery." Portions of the cloister still exist, along with parts of a chapter house built in the 12th century.

Monasterboice
Take the N51 east to the N1. Take the N1 north of Drogheda for about six miles. Watch for the first Dunleer exit north of Drogheda, then follow the signs to Monasterboice. Note: Monasterboice is not signed particularly well from the N1, but watch for the forlorn round tower off the west side of the N1 and make your way over to it. No admission fee; just park your car in the small carpark across the street, and let yourself in the gate.

This site offers one of the premier exhibits of finely preserved high crosses in Ireland. It is the monastic settlement of Monasterboice, which takes its name from the Irish *Mainstir Buithe*, which means "St. Buithe's Abbey." St. Buithe founded a monastery on this site during the 5th century. In 1097, the round tower suffered a devastating fire, destroying the monastic library that was stored there for safekeeping. The monastery was eventually abandoned in the 12th century. The site consists of the ruins of two churches, a round tower, and three high crosses.

Two of the high crosses at Monasterboice are among the best examples of high crosses in the world. One of them, the **Cross of Muiredach**, is remarkably well preserved. An inscription at the base says, "A prayer for Muiredach by whom this cross was made." This 10th-century High Cross stands almost 17 feet tall, and has scenes depicting Adam and Eve, Cain and Abel, Christ as the Judge, and Michael weighing souls. It also contains a depiction of the crucifixion. **Tall Cross** (21 feet high) depicts the sacrifice of Isaac by Abraham, the Vigil at the Tomb, Judas' kiss of betrayal, and the crucifixion. One other cross, the **North Cross**, only partially survived the years. Scholars speculate that these crosses served more than an artistic outlet for some sculptor; they believe the crosses were used by monks to teach their non-reading followers about the scriptures.

The forlorn **round tower** that keeps a silent vigil over Monasterboice is nearly 110 feet tall, even without its peaked cap, which was lost many centuries ago. There is also a six-foot tall granite sundial enclosed with a railing that is interesting to see. In 1979, Monasterboice hosted a visit from Pope John Paul.

Hill of Tara

Near Navan. From Monasterboice, back-track a bit by heading south on the N1 to the N51, then head west to the N2. Once you hit the N2, head south toward Dublin. About eight miles south of Navan, watch for signs directing you to the Hill of Tara. Open May through mid-June daily from 10am to 5pm, mid-June through mid-September daily from 9:30am to 6:30pm, and mid-September through October daily from 10am to 5pm. Admission is €2 for adults, €1.50 for seniors and students, €1 for children and a family ticket is available for €5.

The Hill of Tara is one of the most significant historic, religious, secular, and mythical sights in Ireland. It is the ancient site of the coronation of the Celtic kings of Ireland. Every three years a great *feis* (pronounced *fesh*), or large assembly, was held to pass laws, regulate trade, settle disputes, and forge alliances among the kings of Ireland. It was revered through the centuries as a place of awe.

Atop this legendary hill is a **statue of St. Patrick**, and a small pillar called the *Lia Fial*, the stone believed to have been used as an ancient **coronation stone**. Legend has it that when the High King of Ireland (called the *Ard Ri*) was crowned at this sight, if the coronation was acceptable to the pagan gods, the Lia Fial roared mightily. The pagan Celtic kings

would probably roll over in their graves if they knew the statue of this zealous Christian missionary had been erected on the hill of their ancient coronations.

Today, little else is on the Hill of Tara except grass-covered mounds and the occasional grazing sheep – the new kings of Tara.

DAY TRIP TWO: COUNTY WICKLOW
Featured Sights: Lower Lough Bray, Lough Tay, Glenmacnass Waterfall, Glendalough.

One of our favorite things about getting out to County Wicklow is the drive. It gives you a taste of the "real" Ireland: the green, rolling hills, the stone fences, the sheep, and the cows. If you don't want to drive, there are day-trip bus and van tours to Wicklow available; just keep your eyes open for the fliers at the airports, hotels, or any Dublin tourism center.

Several tour companies offer day trips to Glendalough, but the one we'll share here is offered by **St. Kevin's Bus Service** *(Tel. (01) 281-8119)*, a family-owned Irish bus line:
- 11:30am – depart Dublin from St. Stephen's Green West
- 1:00pm – arrive Glendalough

St. Kevin's buses return from Glendalough in the afternoon and early in the morning (if you choose to spend the night), but here is a schedule that will give you time to tour the visitors' center as well as see all there is to see at Glendalough, and return to Dublin before it gets too late:
- 4:30pm – depart Glendalough
- 5:50pm – arrive Dublin at St. Stephen's Green West

If, however, you prefer to drive, head west out of Dublin to the M50. Go south on the M50 and watch for the R115 (also

Tour Operator Tip

There are numerous tour operators plying their trade in and around Dublin. One tour operator we found to be among the most reasonably priced and enjoyable was **Over the Top Tours**, *Tel. (01) 838-6128*. They offer tours to Wicklow, Glendalough, Newgrange and other locations.

known at this point as Stocking Road). Head south to Glencree. Follow the R115 south as it winds through the Wicklow Mountains. Follow the R115 south right into Laragh and Glendalough.

The first thing you see upon leaving Dublin and entering the Wicklow Mountains is **Lower Lough Bray**. This little lake seemed almost mysterious as it sat serenely shrouded in fog.

Many well-known movies were filmed on the plains you pass on the drive to Wicklow: among them *Braveheart* (and you thought Braveheart was filmed in Scotland! Well, *parts* of it were….), *Saving Private Ryan*, and *King Arthur*. Ireland is a popular place to film movies because if an individual lives in Ireland for at least 150 days while filming the movie, he or she is not taxed on the movie's profits.

You will soon come to **Lough Tay**, better known as Guinness Lake because of its dark brown color. But don't get your hopes up; it gets that color because of all the peat moss on its borders, not because it is a secret storage facility for the Guinness Brewery! As you continue your drive, be sure to notice the tiny city of Annamoe, reportedly the only town in Ireland with no pub!

The next natural beauty on your tour is **Glenmacnass Waterfall**. We have glaciers to thank for this lovely site, as they carved out this waterfall about 9,000 years ago. If you're lucky you will see Glenmacnass Waterfall after a couple of days of rain; it will be spectacular!

Glendalough
In the 6th century **St. Kevin** sought refuge from the world and founded a hermitage here. It is easy to see why. At the west end of the valley, Glenealo Stream cascades in a waterfall into the valley. Two lakes grace Glendalough with their elegance

and beauty. They are called simply **Upper Lake** and **Lower Lake**. Heavily forested mountains encircle the valley, making you feel secluded and safe.

There are also the ruins of the **monastery** St. Kevin built. Of the seventy remaining round monastic towers in Ireland, Glendalough's is the best preserved. It was built as a lookout for Vikings, who found monasteries an easy target for their infamous raids, being guarded by only the peaceful monks themselves. Monasteries were also profitable places to raid, as many people would give their valuables to the monks for safekeeping.

Take your time walking around the ancient gravestones and ruined churches. This area used to be called "The Valley of the Seven Churches" and you will find the ruins of seven churches here, which explains this nickname. Glendalough also boasts a relatively new **visitors' center**, which is about a two-minute walk from the ruins.

If you have driven to Glendalough, let's take a slightly different route back to Dublin and see more stunning views of the Wicklow Mountains. From Glendalough, take the R756 due west to the tiny town of **Hollywood**. An Irishman from Hollywood, Ireland moved to the United States and got rich in the 1840s gold rush. It was he who, out of nostalgia for home, gave California's Hollywood its name. Who knew?

Just past Hollywood, catch the N81 north into Dublin.

DAY TRIP THREE: SOUTHWEST IRELAND
Featured Sights: Blarney Castle and the Blarney Stone, and the Rock of Cashel

If you wish (and if you have the time and the inclination), you can very easily see Blarney on a day trip from Dublin. There are those who feel their trip to Ireland simply wouldn't be complete until they've kissed the **Blarney Stone**.

The Blarney Stone is to be found at the village and castle of the same name, and all three are about five miles north of Cork City. By looking at a map of Ireland, you will quickly discern that it looks like a long way from Dublin. The fact is, it is about a three-and-a-half hour drive from Dublin, or about a four-and-a-half hour bus ride if you prefer not to rent a car. If you decide to take a bus, there are many options available to you. Here is **Bus Eireann's** schedule, for example:

• 8am – depart Busaras Store Street Station in Dublin
• 12:25pm – arrive Cork City Parnell Street Station
• 1:25pm – depart Cork City Parnell Street Station for Blarney
• 1:55pm – arrive Blarney Castle

If you want to make a long (but oh-so-enjoyable) day of it, you can tour the castle, stone and small town of Blarney, then return to Dublin on the same day:

• 5:30pm – depart Blarney
• 5:50pm – arrive Cork City Parnell Street Station
• 6pm – depart Cork City Parnell Street Station
• 10:30pm – arrive Busaras Store Street Station in Dublin

If you want to spend the night, either in Blarney or Cork and return the following day, here's an example of when and where to catch a bus:

• 8:10am – depart Blarney
• 8:45am – arrive Cork City Parnell Street Station
• 10am – depart Cork City Parnell Street Station
• 2:25pm – arrive Busaras Store Street Station in Dublin

If you prefer renting a car and driving, we heartily suggest it. Your journey to Blarney will take you through the heart of **southwest Ireland** – a beautiful drive indeed. If you are on foot in Dublin, take a bus to the airport, and rent your car there. From the airport, catch the M50 south to the M8 and head southwest. At Portlaoise (pronounced Port-leesh'), take the N7 southwest until you come to Cashel.

Let's detour here from your trip to Blarney and check out one of the most picturesque ruins in Ireland – the Rock of Cashel. Cashel is a bustling town that has grown up around the mighty Rock of Cashel. In my mind's eye, I can see this town as the place of habitation for the serfs, smithies, coopers, and tanners who served their masters who resided upon the Rock of Cashel hundreds of years ago. The town has truly grown up around the Rock of Cashel, but continues to render obeisance to it, as it now supports the many tourists who come to pay homage at this sight, just as nobles and clerics have done for hundreds of years.

Rock of Cashel

Cashel. Open mid-March to mid-June daily from 9:30am to 5:30pm, mid-June to mid-September daily from 9am to 7:30pm, and mid-September through mid-March daily from 9:30am to 4:30pm. Admission is €4.50 for adults, €3.50 for seniors and students, €1.90 for children, and a family ticket is available for €10. Last admission is 45 minutes prior to closing. Tel. (062) 61437.

Save plenty of film for one of the most awe-inspiring sites in Ireland. The setting for this chapel/round tower/cathedral is on a mound towering some 200 feet above the surrounding plains (the peak of the round tower is nearly 300 feet above the surrounding plain). The ruins are amazingly well preserved, and the visitors' center at the foot of the Rock of Cashel is informative. Incredible views of the surrounding Tipperary plains await visitors to the site.

Local legend has it that one day the devil was flying over

Ireland. As he approached the Slieve Bloom Mountains, rather than fly over them, he opted to bite a chunk out of them. (Locals will be happy to point out the missing section in the nearby mountains. It's called Devil's Bit.) Displeased with the taste, he spat the earth out here north of Cashel Town. It's this mound of dirt that the structures of the Rock of Cashel have their foundation upon.

The Rock of Cashel (also called St. Patrick's Rock) long held a position of prominence in the history of Ireland. It was used for the coronation of Munster kings from 370 until 1100. The Brian Boru was crowned here. In 1101, the site was given to the Church by An O'Brien,

and it was dedicated "to God, St. Patrick, and St. Ailbhe." A little over two decades later, Bishop Cormac MacCarthy began construction on **Cormac's Chapel**. It can still be seen, and is a fine example of the Romanesque architecture used. Whether you experience bright sunshine, a dull day or a bit of rain while at the Rock of Cashel, is still well worth the visit. Personally, we find that the lowering clouds give the ruins a bit of a mysterious and brooding quality. So regardless of the weather, visit this important and awe-filled site.

The Rock of Cashel has hosted many important events, religious as well as secular. One of the most important was St. Patrick's baptism of **King Aengus**. The story is told that in 450 AD as St. Patrick was preparing to baptize the good king, he tripped and planted his staff rather forcibly into the earth to maintain his balance. After the ceremony, it was discovered that the staff had instead pierced the king's foot, and the grass underneath was moistened by the king's blood. The king hadn't cried out or brought attention to St. Patrick's error, as he thought the pain and suffering were part of the ceremony.

St. Patrick's Cathedral is particularly impressive. Now roofless, it is nonetheless easy to see the grandeur this splendid structure once represented. At the corners of the nave and transepts, spiral staircases run up, up, and up (127 steps) in small round towers up to roof-walks. Connected to the cathedral is the well-preserved round tower, which is 92 feet tall. Its door is 12 feet above the ground. The round tower was built in the early 12th century. During the summer months, the Rock of Cashel is besieged with tourists, but it is still well worth your time to stop and spend some time here.

Okay – after your short detour at Cashel – let's continue your trip to Blarney. Back on the N7, head southwest out of Cashel. As you approach Cork city, catch the N25 west toward Cork. Watch for signs directing you to Blarney, and follow those signs. They will put you on the N20 – the last leg of your jaunt to Blarney.

Blarney Castle & Blarney Stone
Blarney. Open in May on Monday through Saturday from 9am to 6:30pm, June through August Monday through Saturday from 9am to 7pm, September Monday through Saturday from 9am to 6:30pm, and October through April Monday through Saturday from 9am until sundown. They are also open year round on Sunday from 9:30am to 5:30pm. Admission is €8 for adults, 6 for students and senior citizens and €2.50 for children (children under 8 are free). There is a family ticket available for €18.50 (two adults and two children under 14). Last admission is 30 minutes prior to closing. Tel. (021) 438-5252.

Five miles north of Cork City is the town of Blarney and its famous stone. Before our first visit to Ireland, we had no idea the Blarney *Stone* was part of Blarney *Castle*. The famous stone is located atop the ancient keep underneath its battlements.

To kiss the **stone** – which legend says grants the kisser the gift of blarney (flattery) – you lay on your back and slide down and under the battlements. One or two local men are positioned to give you a hand. (May we suggest that you tip them? After all, they do keep you from falling on your head!) One hundred and twenty-ish steps up a spiral staircase will precede your kiss of the Blarney Stone. The castle and surrounding grounds are delightful. During the summer months, the climb to the top of Blarney Castle can be exasperating at times, as *ascending* tourists battle with *descending* tourists for right-of-way on the same narrow circular staircases. However, the views from the top of the keep, not to mention the smooch of the stone, are well worth the wait and effort. Verdant lawns, lovely trees, and a serene streamlet all add to the majesty of the moment.

Cormac McCarthy, Lord of Blarney Castle, was a renowned negotiator and flatterer. On one occasion, an exasperated Queen Elizabeth I declared of McCarthy's honeyed words and

Restaurant and B&B Tip

MACKEY'S RESTAURANT
The Square, Blarney. Tel. (021) 538-5261.
Mackey's is a nice family restaurant on The Square in Blarney. This smallish restaurant offers a variety of fish and beef dinners as well as a nice selection of soups, salads and sandwiches. The menu changes frequently, but you might find such delicacies as stuffed pork steak served with the chef's special creamy mushroom sauce, or a poached salmon steak.

CLARAGH HOUSE
Waterloo Road, Blarney, County Cork. Tel. (021) 488-6308, www.claragh.com. 4 rooms, 3 ensuite. Singles: €28-32, Doubles: €40-45 per person sharing.
It is truly difficult to say which is the loveliest: the Claragh House or your hostess Cecilia Kiely. Claragh House B&B is relatively new, and the rooms are simply and tastefully decorated in pastels with complementing floral wallpaper. Depending on how far in advance you call, you can choose between a blue, pink, or green room. In addition to having a TV to meditate in front of after your day of touring, the sitting room has a nice large window that looks out onto the green Irish countryside.

crafty negotiations: "This is nothing but Blarney - what he says, he never means!"

Almost lost in the excitement of kissing the Blarney Stone is **Blarney Castle** itself. A massive square keep, it stands now as a mere shell of the impressive structure it must have been in its younger days. Its history, like so many other castles in Ireland, is pock-marked with sieges, attacks, and burnings. Cromwell visited here, as did William of Orange after the Battle of the Boyne. (Hint: they didn't come for afternoon tea.)

Blarney is small, with a population about 2,000, but its ranks swell during the summer months as visitors from all over the world descend upon it. Depending on the time of year you are there, you'll encounter from one to scores of tour buses, each one disgorging tourists of all shapes and sizes who have come to one of the most popular (and obligatory!) sights in Ireland.

Now if you have done as we have suggested on this day trip, you will have a very full day indeed. If you drive straight through to Blarney without pausing in Cashel, your journey will take about four hours one way, more or less. If you stop in Cashel and see the ruins there, your journey to Blarney will take about six hours. If you take two hours checking out Blarney Castle and Blarney Stone and walking around the small town, you will have had a long day indeed. You can either drive home – another four hours or so, or you may want to spend the night. See our sidebar on the previous page for our top suggestion for an overnight stay, as well as a good place to eat.

3. PLANNING YOUR TRIP

ACCOMMODATIONS

In Dublin, you have the full spectrum of lodging from which to choose: from somewhat austere youth hostels to luxurious five-star hotels, and everything in between. We've tried to give you a few selections in each price category. The rates listed are "rack" rates. In the hotel listings, "All major credit cards accepted," means Access, American Express, EuroCard, Mastercard, and Visa. If any one of these is not accepted, we have specifically listed those that are accepted. we have listed a range of rates if the rates vary throughout the year. The lower rates are typically only valid during the off or low seasons, and the higher rates are valid from about June through September.

Ariel House

50-52 Lansdowne Road, Dublin 4. Tel. (01) 668-5512, Fax (01) 668-5845. 40 rooms. Rates for singles: €65-100, doubles: €45-75 per person sharing, suites: €150-200 per person sharing. Call for special rates that are offered from time to time, especially during the winter months. Rates do not include breakfast. Mastercard and Visa accepted. 10% service charge. Three Victorian townhouses, built in the 1850s, have been converted into this award-winning "Best Small Hotel in Ireland." Twenty of the thirty rooms are furnished almost exclusively with furniture from the Victorian era. The rooms range from lovely to elegant. Several miles from downtown Dublin but only 100 yards from the Lansdowne DART station – that is, about a three-minute ride to downtown.

Stauntons on the Green

83 St. Stephen's Green South, Dublin 2. Tel. (01) 478-2300, Fax (01) 478-2263. 38 rooms. Rates for singles: €79-114, doubles: €63-75 per person sharing, suites: €105-130. Rates include breakfast. No service charge. On the south side of St. Stephen's Green, Stauntons is a series of converted Georgian townhouses. From the moment you enter her grand and dignified lobby, you will be delighted when you see how wonderfully the owners have restored the high-ceilinged rooms, which are large and individually decorated with taste and elegance. The rooms at the front of the house overlook St. Stephen's Green and those at the back of the hotel overlook flower gardens.

Albany House Bed and Breakfast

84 Harcourt Street, Dublin 2. Tel. (01) 475-1092, Fax (01) 475-1093; Web: www.byrne-hotels-ireland.com. 33 rooms. Rates for singles: €73-79, doubles: €70-77 per person sharing. All major credit cards accepted. No restaurant. No service charge. Albany House is one of the finest examples of Georgian architecture in Dublin. Built in the late 18th century, it was once part of the estate of the Earl of Clonmel. The bedrooms are spacious and are comfortably and expensively furnished. The high ceilings accentuate the spaciousness of the rooms, and the tall windows let plenty of light into each room.

Shelbourne Meridien Hotel

27 St. Stephen's Green, Dublin 2. Tel. (01) 663-4500, Fax (01) 661-6006; Web: www.shelbourne.ie. 190 rooms. Rates for singles: €307-329, doubles: €307-391, and suites: €559-1,400. One restaurant and two bars. All major credit cards accepted. 15% service charge. The Shelbourne receives my vote for the nicest of the nice in Dublin. From the rich dark wood to the lovely antique Waterford crystal chandelier in the Lord Mayor's lounge to the flawless service, this is a superb place to stay. The Shelbourne has undergone extensive renovations and is an even better hotel than it was previously.

Westbury Hotel

Grafton Street, Dublin 2. Tel. (01) 679-1122, Fax (01) 679-7078, US toll free 800/423-6953; Web: www.jurys.com/ireland/ doyle_westbury.htm. 190 rooms. Rates for singles: €269-356, doubles: €269-395, suites: €300-700. Two restaurants and one bar, fitness center. All major credit cards accepted. 15% service charge. One of the brightest gems in the Doyle Hotel Group tiara. The contemporary lobby, decorated in cream and red marble with brass and crystal aplenty, lets you know you've made a grand selection. The rooms are smallish by American

standards, but lavishly decorated. The modern furniture is almost plush. The junior and senior suites are much nicer.

Cherry wood desks and tables add to the rich and extravagant setting. Another plus is the location: just a half block off Grafton Street (even though their address is given as Grafton Street), it is in the hub of activity in Dublin. Free parking for guests is included.

Longfield's Hotel

10 Fitzwilliam Street Lower. Tel. (01) 676-1367, Fax (01) 676-1542; Web: www.longfields.ie. 28 rooms. Rates for singles: €99-135, doubles: €99-165. One restaurant. All major credit cards accepted. No service charge. Lovely comfortable rooms, a

safe neighborhood, a great location close to shopping and sights, and personable, outgoing staff. This is one of the nicest small hotels in Dublin.

Conrad Hotel

Earlsfort Terrace, Dublin 2. Tel. (01) 676-5555, Fax (01) 676-5424, US toll free 800/Hilton, Web: conradhotels1.hilton.com. 191 rooms. Rates for singles: €200-450, doubles: €230-490, suites: €400-1,100. Two restaurants and one pub. All credit cards accepted. 15% service charge. Part of the Hilton Hotels group. From its glimmering marble and brass lobby to its ultra-luxurious Presidential Suite, everything is top quality. The rooms are ample size, and very nicely decorated with quality furnishings and pleasant decor. The Conrad is also one of the few hotels in Ireland that is air conditioned. Rooms in the front of the hotel overlook the National Concert Hall across the street. The suites are spacious and lavish, and are among the nicest in all of Ireland.

Burlington Hotel

Upper Leesom Street, Ballsbridge, Dublin 4. Tel. (01) 660-5222, Fax (01) 660-5064, US toll free 800/448-8355; Web: www.jurys.com/ireland/doyle_burlington. 503 rooms. Rates for singles: €180, doubles: €109-250, suites: €400. Two restaurants, one lounge and one pub. All major credit cards accepted. 15% service charge. Crystal chandeliers, marble and brass, dark wood and plush carpet all welcome you with surprising warmth and gaiety as you enter the lobby of the hotel. The rooms are large and bright, and the furnishings are top quality. The bathrooms are similarly luxurious. The suites are expansive and lavish and filled with lovely, comfortable furnishings.

Berkeley Court Hotel

Lansdowne Road, Ballsbridge, Dublin 4. Tel. (01) 660-1711, Fax: (01) 497-8275, US toll free 800/638-0006; Web: www.jurys.com/ireland/doyle_berkeley_court. 200 rooms. Rates for singles/doubles: €300; suites: €345-725; Penthouse Suite: €1,600. Two restaurants and a lounge. All major credit cards accepted. 15% service charge. If you want plush, elegant, and a wee bit of the extraordinary, the Berkeley Court Hotel is the place to stay. There is rich dark paneling in the Royal Court Bar and a serene elegance in the Berkeley Room restaurant. The rooms are large and equally as inviting and luxurious as the public rooms. Decorated in soft pastels, the rooms are light and airy, with comfortable, classic furniture.

Oliver St. John Gogarty's Youth Hostel

18-21 Anglesea Street, Dublin 2. Tel. (01) 671-1822, Fax (01) 671-7637; Web: www.olivergogartys.com. 27 rooms, 130 beds. Rates for twins: €23-28 per person sharing, three beds: €21-25 per person sharing, four beds: €19-23 per person sharing, dormitory: €18-23 per person sharing. One cafe. American Express, Mastercard, and Visa accepted. No service charge. This is one of the newest and nicest youth hostels in Ireland, with new plumbing, comfortable (albeit bunk) beds, and clean linens. Good location in the trendy, up-and-coming Temple Bar District, Dublin's answer to Paris's Left Bank.

Avalon House Youth Hostel

55 Aungier Street, Dublin 2. Tel. (01) 475-0001, Fax (01) 475-0303; Web: www.avalon-house.ie. 185 beds. Rates for singles: €30-37 per person sharing, twins: €28-35 per person sharing, four beds: €20-30 per person sharing, dormitory: €15-30 per person sharing (rates include light continental breakfast). One cafe. American Express, Mastercard, and Visa accepted. Cafe on site. No service charge. Probably the busiest hostel in Dublin and offers the most amenities as well. There is a small cafe, a

Bureau de Change, self-catering kitchen facilities, laundry service, TV room, luggage storage, and secure bicycle storage.

ARRIVALS & DEPARTURES

Dublin International Airport, *Tel. (01) 705-2222*, is about six miles north of Dublin's city center. It is the principal airport for flights from Europe, England, Scotland, and the United States. The airport code is DUB. Transatlantic flights to Ireland from the US land in Dublin (some flights land in Shannon first, then continue on to Dublin). Canadian passengers flying to Dublin or Shannon must connect in Chicago, Boston, New York, or London.

From the airport to Dublin's city center you can choose a taxi, bus, express bus, or rental car.

Getting to Town By Taxi

The taxi stand is just outside the doors of the Arrivals Hall. If you hire a taxi, the 25-minute ride from the airport will cost you around €20 including tip, and is certainly the quickest way to get into town.

Getting to Town by Bus

You have two choices for a bus ride into the city: express or regular bus. The **express bus** gets you into town nearly as quickly as does a taxi, but at a considerably lower cost. The 25-minute ride costs €5. It can take about 15 minutes longer during rush hour. The express bus takes you into the heart of Dublin, stopping at **Busaras Station** *(Tel. 01 836-6111, Store Street)* in the O'Connell Street District north of the River Liffey. It also stops just beyond the main Tourist Information office in Dublin, just off Grafton Street. The service runs daily every half hour from 7:30am to 11pm.

To catch the express bus, turn left coming out of the Arrivals Hall, and walk about 100 feet to bus stop #1.

To catch the **regular bus** into the city from the airport, go about 50 feet further than the express bus stop to bus stop #2. This bus stops all along the way into downtown Dublin, but it only costs €1.90. It takes 30 minutes longer without heavy traffic, but will take you to any number of places in downtown Dublin – but not to Busaras, the main bus station.

GETTING AROUND DUBLIN
By Bicycle
Bicycling is an excellent way to see Dublin, and there are many bicycle rental shops in the city from which to rent a bicycle. Rates average about €10 per day and €50 per week, and most bike shops require a deposit, usually €30-40. In fact, there is a bike rental shop, called **Rent-a-Bike**, right around the corner from the Busaras station, at the corner of Lower Gardener Street and French Lane.

Use caution. The main thoroughfares in the city are often congested with traffic, especially at rush hour. However, once you get out of the heart of the city, bicycling is quite pleasant.

By Bus
Buses crisscross the city on a regular basis, and are relatively inexpensive. Fares are charged based on distance to your destination, from €0.80-2.40. You may purchase your ticket from the bus driver – but you'll need exact change. If you are going to be in Dublin for a few days and intend on using the bus to get around, you will probably be money ahead to purchase a one-day ticket for €5, a three-day ticket for €10 or a five-day ticket for €15.

The buses run regularly from 6:30am (9:30am on Sundays) until 11:30pm each night. You can catch the bus at any number of stops in the city. Most routes begin at or near O'Connell Bridge and **bus starters** at O'Connell bridge will be more than happy to point you to the correct bus stop. (Bus-starters are bus company employees at the O'Connell Street station whose job it is to make sure individuals – especially tourists – get on the right bus.)

If you are planning to use the bus, get a map since O'Connell Bridge may not be convenient. If you are on the outskirts of the city, just look for the bus destination signs that say *An Lar*, Irish for "the center."

By Car

Traffic in Dublin is a good reason to leave your rental car parked. Better yet, save yourself a few euros and don't rent a car unless you are going to take one or more of the day trips we have suggested. Drivers in Dublin are maniacal. Add to their craziness aggressive motorcyclists and daring pedestrians, and you'll be tempted to turn in your AAA card and international driver's license if you try to drive in Dublin!

If you do choose to drive in Dublin, you will assuredly be parking. Parking rules are a little different than in the United States, and sometimes the rules are not intuitively obvious. Bear the following tip in mind.

It is illegal to park:
• within five meters of an intersection
• at a taxi stand or bus stop
• where there is a continuous white line, unless the roadway has at least three traffic lanes
• in such a manner as to cause an obstruction
• within 15 meters of the approach side of a crosswalk, or within five meters on the other side of a crosswalk
• when double yellow lines are present; if a single yellow line is present, it is illegal to park from 8:30am to 6:30pm, Monday through Friday

Dublin has a parking system called **Disk Parking** in the city center. This fact is generally prominently displayed throughout the parts of the city where disk parking is required. *Do not ignore these signs.* If you do, you may find yourself the proud owner of a €20 parking ticket. (Do we sound as though we are speaking from experience?!) Parking disks can be purchased at any Newsagent for the modest sum of €0.75, and are very wise investments. These cards have a series of months, days, and years, as well as hours and minutes on them. When you find a parking place in a disk zone, park your car. Before you leave, scratch off the correct day, month, and year, as well as the correct hour and minute. Place the completed parking disk on the inside of the curb-side window.

Check the signs near your parking place for the maximum amount of time you can park with a parking disk – it is usually an hour or two. If the maximum period is two hours, you must complete two parking disks and have both displayed in your window. Once the maximum time has expired, you must move your car from that street for at least one hour. Each parking disk generally has instructions for its use on the back of the disk. While Ireland is very tuned into tourists and tourism, there seems to be no hesitation to ticket rental cars for failing to follow the parking rules of the city!

By Foot

I believe you can comfortably see most of Dublin's sights on foot. Dublin is a very easy city to get around. Most of the interesting sights are within a relatively compact area, and well within walking distance.

Most of the major streets in Dublin are wide and easy to negotiate, and many of them are one-way. They have come up with a unique way to protect people who come from countries where they drive on the right-hand side of the road. As you step off the curb at cross-walks, written on the road in big bold letters are the words LOOK TO THE RIGHT - > or < - LOOK TO THE LEFT, depending on which side of the street you're on and whether you are on a one-way or two-way street.

By Taxi

There are several **taxi stands** throughout the city: the airport, the Busaras station, Connolly, Pearse, and Heuston train stations, on O'Connell Street, College Green (in front of the Bank of Ireland), and St. Stephen's Green North. You can also call a cab company and have a taxi pick you up, although there is usually an additional charge (€2-4) to have them do so. In the past you couldn't hail a taxi in Dublin, but that is changing. While I have witnessed numerous unsuccessful attempts to hail empty on-duty taxis when I was last in Dublin, I also saw a few stop and pick up passengers who hailed them.

Taxi service in Dublin is efficient and relatively inexpensive. However, unless you are going outside of the immediate downtown area, you're just as well off walking. In the event you decide to take a cab, here are the numbers of several taxi companies in Dublin:

- A1 Taxis, *Tel. (01) 285-9333*
- Blue Cabs, *Tel. (01) 676-1111*
- Capital Cabs, *Tel. (01) 490-8888*
- Central Cabs, *Tel. (01) 836-5555*
- City Group, *Tel. (01) 872-7272*
- Metro Cabs, *Tel. (01) 668-3333*

By Train

The **Dublin Area Rapid Transit (DART)** is an electrified train that reaches from Dublin's city center to outlying communities as far north as Howth and as far south as Bray. It runs every 15 minutes (every five minutes during rush hours) from 6:30am until 11:30pm. If you are heading north on the DART, you need to be on the west platform, and if you are headed south, you should be on the east platform. These green trains are models of efficiency that zip their passengers to their destinations swiftly and relatively quietly. DART has a well-deserved reputation for timeliness, and you can practically set your watch by it. Fares are reasonable and distance-dependent. You can purchase an all-day DART pass for €3.20 if you plan to ride it for more than just a few trips. There is no smoking on DART and the fine for doing so is €400!

At some stations you may feel a moment's disorientation due to the use of a common word in an uncommon manner. Watch for signs directing you to the "subway." This is not an underground train with which you may be familiar, but rather a "subterranean walkway" that takes you under the tracks to the exit. If you are really confused, just follow the crowds, or ask someone.

The DART stations are: Howth, Sutton, Bayside, Howth Junction, Kilbarrack, Raheny, Harmonstown, Killester, Connolly, Tara Street, Pearse, Lansdowne Road, Sandymount, Sidney Parade, Booterstown, Blackrock, Seapoint, Monkstown, Dun Laoghaire, Sandycove, Glenageary, Dalkey, Killiney, Shankill, and Bray.

BASIC INFORMATION
Climate & Weather

Ireland enjoys a temperate climate year-round, thanks to the warm waters of the Gulf Stream. Most tourists find the weather pleasant and more than acceptable for vacationing from April through October, although we have been there in the winter months and found it to be delightful as well, although a wee bit chilly.

During **April -May**, the temperatures are generally in the high 40s to mid-50s Fahrenheit during the days. During the **summer** months, you can expect the temperatures to be in the 60s, with even an occasional day or two in the 70s. **Fall** temperatures generally emulate those of the springtime, with daytime temperatures ranging from the high 40s to mid-50s most of the time. For the most part, **winters** on the Emerald Isle are also mild, with average temperatures in the mid-30s to low 40s.

But beware! There is a reason Ireland is known as the Emerald Isle. There are more shades of green than you can count, and they remain that way due to the frequency of **rain**, which can be anytime, anywhere throughout the year. (The average annual rainfall in Ireland is 43 inches.) However, despite frequent rain showers, it seldom rains hard enough to dampen the enjoyment of the many sights there are to see. We've found that a sweater (purchased in Ireland, of course), a lightweight raincoat, and (perhaps) an umbrella will make your touring pleasant.

July and August are the peak tourist months in Dublin, and it is during these months that you may find yourself waiting in line to see some of the more popular sights such as the Book of Kells. During April, May, September and October, the numbers of tourists are noticeably less, and during the winter months you're liable to be downright lonely for the company of fellow travelers.

Dublin has plenty of "dull days" – the Irish term for overcast or cloudy days. But other than providing an opaque backdrop for most of your photographs, there's really no harm done by the dull days. But oh – when the sky is a shimmering blue it is a sight to behold!

The Emerald Isle has Daylight Savings Time – called Summer Time. It begins the last Sunday of March, and reverts to Standard Time the last Sunday in October. This is a complimentary bonus of extra daylight hours with which to continue your walks around the city, or an extra hour or two to prowl around any pubs that catch your eye.

Business Hours
Businesses are generally open from 9am to 5pm, Monday through Saturday (some stores stay open until 6pm on Saturday), although in practice most stores open at 9:30am or 10am. In Dublin, some stores will stay open later one night of the week. Also, on our last visit, we noticed that about 20% of the stores in the main shopping districts were open on Sunday from about noon to 6pm, a trend we expect will catch on.

Banking & Changing Money
On January 1, 2002, along with 11 other members of the European Union (EU), Ireland embraced a new international currency – the **Euro (€)**. At the time of this writing, the conversion rate has been in the neighborhood of US$1.20 to $1.25 and CD$1.50 to CD$1.65 for each euro (€1). To find out what the current conversion rate is before your trip, the power of the Internet allows you to do so within a moment's notice by going to *www.xe.com/ucc.* There are a number of currency converters on the web, but we have found this one to be the easiest to use. If you do not have internet access, then you may call any sizable bank, AAA, currency exchange office or look at the Foreign Exchange box in the business section of your local newspaper.

The euro uses the same numbering schemes as US and Canadian dollars. But instead of dollars and cents, you'll find euros and cents. Euro coins come in the following denominations: €2 and €1 euro coins, and 50-, 20-, 10-, 5-, 2- and 1-cent coins.

If you forget or can't get to a bank or currency exchange office to exchange your money before you leave, don't worry. There are currency exchange kiosks in most gateway city airports (Chicago, Boston, New York, and Atlanta), as well as at the Shannon and Dublin airports. You'll have to pay a minimal service charge, usually around $5.

Banks in Dublin are open…well…they're open banker's hours. Traditionally, banks in Dublin are open Monday through Wednesday and Friday from 10am to 12:30pm, and from 1:30pm to 4pm. On Thursdays their *extended* hours are from 10am to 12:30pm and 1:30pm to 5pm. The bank in the Dublin airport, however, is open every day to service incoming international flights. Post offices in Dublin will also exchange money for you. Be aware, however, that they will not accept $100 bills. Some larger hotels will also change money for you.

Automatic Teller Machines (ATMs) are nowhere near as ubiquitous as in America; they can usually be found on the outside wall of banks. Cirrus and Plus are the international networks most of these ATMs are part of. Most of the banks that provide ATMs charge a small transaction fee for withdrawals (about $1.50). Check with the bank that issued your ATM card to see if your current Personal Identification Number (PIN) will work overseas. Many of the ATMs overseas only accept four-digit PINs.

Electricity
Electricity in Ireland is **220 volts** (50 cycles) and an adapter is required. Most discount stores like Target, K-Mart, and Wal-Mart, as well as Sears and J.C. Penny's carry inexpensive adapters that will do the job nicely. Remember, if you expect to use your hair dryer, curling iron, or electric razor, you'll need an adapter. Oh yes – and unless you're going to bring lots of very expensive (and heavy) batteries, you'll want that adapter to recharge the batteries for your video recorder and digital camera (common oversights).

Embassies & Consulates

• U.S. Embassy, *42 Elgin Road, Dublin 4, Tel. (01) 668-8777.* Open Monday through Friday from 8:30am to 5pm.

• British Embassy, *29 Merrion Road, Dublin 4. Tel. (01) 205-3700.* Open Monday through Friday from 8:30am to 4:30pm.

• Canadian Embassy, *65 St. Stephen's Green, Tel. (01) 478-1988.* Open Monday through Wednesday from 8:30am to 12:30pm, and from 2pm to 4pm, and Thursday and Friday from 8:30am to 12:30pm.

Health

Before you leave for your holiday in Ireland, check with your health insurance company to see if you will be covered in the event of an emergency, illness, or injury during your travels in Ireland. If you are covered, find out the procedure they require you to follow before seeking treatment. As you may know, both Ireland and Northern Ireland have national health care systems, and unless you have insurance, you will only be treated in the event of an emergency. As of this writing, Medicare doesn't cover overseas medical expenses, but some of their supplemental plans do. Check before going.

Public Holidays

Most offices and stores are closed on the following public holidays in Dublin:

• January 1 – New Year's Day
• March 17 – St. Patrick's Day (what did you expect!?)
• Monday following Easter Sunday – Easter Monday
• First Monday in May – May Holiday (most commonly called Bank Holiday)
• First Monday in June – June Holiday (most commonly called Bank Holiday)
• First Monday in August – August Holiday (most commonly called Bank Holiday)
• First Monday in October – October Holiday (most commonly called Bank Holiday)
• December 25 – Christmas Day
• December 26 – St. Stephen's Day

Packing Tips

We've packed for Dublin two ways: heavy and light. On our first trip, we packed for every conceivable weather condition and social occasion. On our next trip, we packed lightly, going for versatile clothing. We're here to tell you the latter method is far superior.

Here are the necessities for a **week's trip**: sweater, 3-4 shirts (usually long sleeve), a couple of pairs of casual-style pants, one skirt for women, comfortable shoes, several pair of underwear and socks. If you plan on eating in the finest restaurants in Ireland (like Restaurant Patrick Guilbaud, for example), of course you'll want to bring a suitable pair of slacks, a suit or sports jacket, and possibly a tie for men, and a nice dress, skirt and blouse, or pants suit and nylons and shoes for women. Children tend to go through their clothes faster, but we recommend you pack clothes comparable to what you pack for yourself, although they may need a few extra changes of clothes.

You can get just about any toiletry you might need in Ireland: toothpaste, deodorant, shampoo, lotion, make-up and feminine care products. You'll have to decide how important your particular brand is to you, because it may not be sold in Ireland. If you require prescription drugs, we recommend you bring enough for your trip, but be sure you know exactly what you take, how often, and in what dose in case you lose your medication. Hair dryers are generally available in most hotels and many B&Bs and guesthouses. If you have to have a hair dryer, you should bring your own, but make sure you also bring a converter and plug adapter.

Passport

First and foremost, you must have a **current passport** to enter Ireland (which of course, you must do to enter Dublin!). If you have traveled internationally, you probably already have one; it's a good idea to check the expiration date *well before* you plan to travel. American passports are valid for five years for children and 10 years for adults. Canadian passports are valid for five years. All US citizens traveling to Ireland must have a valid passport. For Canadian citizens, children under 16 can be included on their parents' passports, but they must have their own passport if they are traveling alone.

If you are getting a new passport, you should apply six weeks before you plan to depart (four weeks in Canada). That should give you plenty of time to receive your passport. If you are inside the six-week window, don't fear – you can still get a passport, but it will be more expensive, as you will have to pay for overnight mail charges. About five days is the quickest you can get a passport, but I wouldn't cut it that short! Applications are available at US or Canadian passport offices as well as at some post offices. Some Canadian travel agencies also have passport applications.

Ireland requires only a passport for entry into their country. No visa is necessary if you are a citizen of the United States, Canada, Australia, or New Zealand and if your stay is less than 90 days (180 days if you are planning a visit to Northern Ireland). If you plan an extended stay that lasts longer than that, you must demonstrate that you have adequate funds to stay and already possess a return airline ticket.

Customs

Americans who have been out of the country for more than 48 hours may return to the US with up to $400 worth of goods without paying duty. In addition, you may return with up to 200 cigarettes and one liter of alcohol (you must be at least 21 years old to bring liquor back). If you are traveling as a family, the exemptions apply to each person, but can be pooled as a group.

If the total value of your purchases is greater than $400, you will be expected to pay additional duty. Currently, you must pay 10% duty on the next $1,000 worth of items you are returning with. Beyond the $1,400 threshold (the $400 duty free and the next $1,000 worth of goods), you will be assessed a fee based on the category your purchases fall into. If you need to pay additional duty, cash, checks, travelers checks, and (in some places) credit cards are acceptable.

Canadians once a year are allowed to bring C$300 worth of foreign goods back home without paying duty. That applies if you have been out of the country for at least seven days. If you have been gone less than seven days, but more than 48 hours, you can bring back C$100 duty-free each trip, and there is no limit to the number of times you can do this. Exemptions apply to all members of a family traveling with you, but the exemptions cannot be combined as a group. You may also bring home, duty-free, 1.14 liters of wine or liquor or twenty-four 12-oz. bottles of beer or ale. If you are 16 years of age or older, you may bring home, also duty-free, 200 cigarettes, 50 cigars or cigarillos, and 400 tobacco sticks or 400 grams of manufactured tobacco.

Both American and Canadian citizens can mail gifts home duty-free if the gifts are valued at less than US$50 and C$60. You can only mail one package per day per addressee. Packages should be marked "Unsolicited gift." Packages should also be marked on the outside with the retail value. The value of these gifts is not part of your exemption, and they are duty-free.

During your return flight home, flight attendants will hand out Customs forms for you to complete. You are expected to declare the total value of all products you bring in with you.

Phrases & Language

Irish is the official language of the Republic of Ireland, with English recognized as a second language under the Constitution. **Gaelic** and **Irish** are generally interchangeable terms, although today the language is almost always referred to as Irish. Gaelic is most often used to refer to the language of the ancient inhabitants of Ireland, the Celts.

During the past century, English was becoming the daily language of the majority of the Irish people, and Irish was becoming a (nearly) dead language. In an effort to combat this, the Gaelic League was formed in 1893. When the Irish state was formed in 1921, the government made the restoration and preservation of the Irish language one of its priorities. To this end, areas where Irish was still the daily language were designated as *Gaeltacht*, and special financial grants were made available to encourage individuals to remain in the largely rural areas. Large parts of counties Donegal, Galway, and Kerry, as well as parts of counties Mayo, Cork, Waterford, and Meath all qualified.

Today, linguists estimate only 5% of the Irish people speak Irish as their primary language. There is a very real concern that the Irish language will die out entirely.

Regional accents abound in Ireland. Around Dublin, the accents tend to have a strong English flavor. In County Cork in the southwest, accents have a more sing-songy quality. In the extreme west, Galway and Donegal in particular, accents are more what Americans expect – quite frankly, the accent you hear on the "Irish Spring" soap commercials! In Northern Ireland, accents have a strong resemblance to a thick Scottish brogue, most likely due to the predominance of Scottish settlers who settled there over the centuries.

While we share a similar language with the Irish, there are some distinct differences. Another difference is that there are still many vestiges of Gaelic in their vocabulary. Many towns and villages retain their ancient Irish names and children are given seemingly unpronounceable Irish names, for example: Aoife, Oísin, and Niamh to name a few.

Below are some of the more common **Irish words** you are certain to encounter during your visit. Many of them are anglicized versions of Irish words – for example, Bally is the anglicized *Baile*, which means "town." Many small towns in Ireland carry the prefix Bally: Ballymena, Ballyconnell, Ballydonegan, Ballydoyle, etc.

- ard — a high place
- ath — ford
- bally — town
- ben — large hill or mountain
- bord — office or board
- burren — stone
- cahir — stone fort
- carrig — rock

- cashel — stone fort
- cavan — cave
- ceile — dance
- derry — oak
- drum — low ridge or mound
- dun — fort
- êireann — Ireland
- feis — feast or celebration
- gal — river
- kil — church
- lough — lake
- mac — son
- mor — great
- quay — pier
- rath — earthen ring fort
- skerry — sea rocks
- slieve — mountain
- tully — small hill

Here are a few common **English words** that will be helpful to know in conversation, since the meanings are sometimes different in Ireland:

- call — visit
- hire — rent
- homely — homey
- on holiday — on vacation
- pram — baby stroller
- plain — down-to-earth
- queue — line
- ring — call on the phone
- tariff — rate (as in the rate for a hotel room)

One last lesson: *Celtic* is pronounced differently than the way we pronounce the name of the NBA team from Boston. The Celtic you see in Ireland is pronounced Keltic, with a hard K, and it was spoken by Kelts. (Not *Seltic* spoken by *Selts*!)

Postal Regulations
Letters and postcards sent from Dublin to the US and Canada cost 55 eurocents. If you have occasion to send them to

Europe, letters and postcards cost 55 cents. Stamps are available from the post office, or from most Newsagents.

Most post offices in Dublin are open Monday through Saturday from 9am to 5:30pm. The General Post Office (GPO) in Dublin has extended ours. They are open Monday - Saturday from 8am to 8pm and Sundays from 10am to 6:30pm.

If you're going to be in Dublin for a time, you can arrange to have your mail sent to a post office in Dublin. They will hold the mail for you free of charge for three months.

Public Restrooms

Public restrooms are not prevalent in Ireland; your best bet is usually a hotel or a pub. Most hotels have at least one pub, and the restrooms are usually located near the pub. A word to the wise: sometimes the doors to public restrooms, even in Dublin, may be labeled in Irish. If you guess, you'll probably guess wrong: *Mna* is for women, and *Fir* is for men. Take heed, lest you experience more of Ireland than you intend.

Shopping

Dublin is a great shopping town. Many shops vie for your business, from the mom-and-pop specialty shops to some of the most sophisticated and up-to-date mall-type shops.

Speaking of mall-type shops, at the south end of Grafton Street, just across from St. Stephen's Green is the **Stephens Green Shopping Centre** – a modern mall with over 100 stores and dining establishments. **Francis Street**, about four blocks west of there, is known as Antiques Row, and it features some fabulous antique stores.

Grafton Street itself is a shopping area, with a wonderful selection of stores and restaurants, and O'Connell Street north of the Liffey is reclaiming it's rights as a premier shopping area. Near O'Connell Street is **Moore Street**, featuring an open-air market for fruits, vegetables and flowers. Even if you don't want to purchase any of those items, take your camera along for some wonderful, vivid shots of life as it has been for many, many years.

The two main department store chains in Dublin are **Cleries** and **Dunn's**. Cleries is front-and-center on O'Connell Street near the Spire of Dublin, and Dunn's has a large store on the south side of the Liffey near the Suffolk Street tourism office.

Safety & Avoiding Trouble

Crime in Ireland is far from non-existent, but the majority of it has tended to be of the non-violent type. Murders in Ireland send shock waves through the country and are always accompanied by front-page headlines and are the lead stories in newscasts. The **Gardi** (police) do not carry weapons, but are all "armed" with radios.

Dublin, like big cities all over the world, seems to be the most susceptible to crime. The majority of the crime there is petty theft and burglaries, although more violent crimes of rape and murder do occur. Throughout Dublin you'll see signs warning you of pickpockets, who work high-traffic areas like the DART stations, and Grafton and Henry streets. Rental cars are also easy targets, especially if you leave purses, cameras, or other items of value in plain sight. Take a few extra seconds and put those things in the trunk of your car.

The streets of downtown Dublin are relatively safe, but there are areas you will definitely want to stay away from. The docks are notorious for crime, as are large areas of apartments (flats) to the west and northeast of the center of Dublin. If you confine your activities to the areas outlined in this guide, you should have no problem. Notwithstanding the relatively low crime rate, don't be lulled into a false sense of security; there are malevolent people in every land who prey upon the innocent and unsuspecting. It would be a shame to spoil a delightful holiday by taking silly chances.

Of course, when traveling on your own you should take some precautions. Let someone back home know your tentative schedule and when you expect to be back, for example. Lone travelers tend to be more of a target than two or more people traveling together. Just be cautious, and use common sense.

Ireland has very aggressive laws when it comes to driving under the influence of alcohol, so be sure and use a designated driver if you plan to imbibe at one of those delightful Irish pubs.

If you do have trouble, remember that in Ireland you call **999**.

Telephones

Unless you are a hermit, in trouble with the law, or trying to lose yourself from the world, you will need to use Alexander Graham Bell's grand invention – the telephone. Be warned: you will not find the same consistent, user-friendly interface you are accustomed to in North America. Without a doubt you will experience uncooperative phones, occasional poor reception, and just plain frustration. It may take you two or three times dialing exactly the same numbers to get a call through, or you may need to deposit your coins two or three times before they'll register. But, with a little patience, you will be able to get your calls placed.

If you think you might need a phone soon, and you see one, use it. Public phones are not as prevalent as they are in the United States. The surest place to find them is in hotels, although this is not always the case in smaller hotels.

These are the **telephone codes** you need to know:
• International Direct Dialing – 011
• International Credit Card – 01
• Ireland – 353
• Dublin City – 01

If you're going **to call Ireland** from the United States to make hotel reservations, you must dial the country code (353 for Ireland; 44 for Northern Ireland), and the city code, then the telephone number. *Sort of.* In the case of Dublin telephone numbers, the city code is 01, but you drop the 0 when dialing from the United States. Therefore, if you were calling the Berkeley Court Hotel from the United States, you should dial 011-353-1-497-8275. (011 is the international long distance direct dialing code; 01 is the international code for credit card calls.) Any time you see a lead zero in a city code, drop that 0 when calling from the United States.

When calling home from Ireland, dial 1-800/550-000 if you're using AT&T, or 1-800/551-001 if you are using MCI. You will be connected to an AT&T or MCI operator in the United States who will help you complete your calling card or collect call.

Some hotels only allow you to place international calls through the operator (111) from their rooms, so you may want to use the pay phone in the lobby or on the street. While not as convenient, it's a lot more reasonable. Also, some hotels levy a surcharge for in-room international calls that can equal what the long distance carriers charge, effectively doubling the cost of your call. If this matters to you, check with the front desk before you make calls from your room.

Cell phones are ubiquitous in the United States. Some carriers have coverage plans that reach Ireland – on a recent trip to Ireland, we were able to call home using our cell phone with Cingular service from virtually the entire country. Check with your carrier before you leave for Ireland to see if you will be able to call from there.

Another option, and one we have found nearly as inexpensive and trouble free as international dialing plans, is to purchase **international phone cards**. The cost for calls to the US range from 10-50¢ per minute. The range varies widely, and those sold at Irish post offices tended to be more expensive per minute than those you purchase at grocery stores of Newsagents. Most of the cards sold now have a toll-free number to call for access, and these can be used from any phone. Instructions on the back of each card walk you through the process of making a phone call.

Useful telephone numbers include the following:
• Emergency 999
• Directory Assistance - National 11811
• Directory Assistance – International 114
• Operator Assistance – National 10

- Dublin Airport – (01) 844-4900
- Shannon Airport – (061) 471-444
- Aer Lingus – (01) 705-6705
- Delta – (01) 844-4170
- Irish Rail passenger info – (01) 836-6222
- DART information – (01) 836-3333
- Bus Eireann – (01) 836-1111
- Dublin Bus – (01) 873-4222
- Irish Ferries – (01) 661-0511
- General Post Office – (01) 872-8888
- Bord Failte Tourist Board – (01) 602-4000

Most of your calls within Ireland will be made from one of two types of public telephones: coin phones or phonecard phones.

Coin phones in Ireland have been updated and will accept only €0.20-0.50 coins. All calls are metered. A digital screen on the phone registers the amount of money you enter, and counts down to 0 as you talk. At 0, you receive three warning tones, and if you do not add additional coins within 10 seconds, your call will be cut off. If you have credits remaining at the end of your call, you can push a button that allows you to make another call without adding additional coins. Unused, whole amounts will be returned to you.

Phonecard phones are becoming increasingly popular in Ireland. Post Offices and Newsagents sell phonecards of varying denominations: €2, €5, €10, €15 and €25. Like the coin phones, once the card is inserted, a digital readout on the phone displays remaining units. On local calls, one unit is roughly equal to three minutes; slightly less for long distance calls, depending on the distance involved. Some of the phone cards now feature a toll-free number to dial, after which you input a PIN associated with that card. These phone cards can be used with any telephones.

Time

Ireland is on Greenwich Mean Time, and for most of the year that means they are five hours ahead of New York and Montreal, and eight hours ahead of Los Angeles and Vancouver. Ireland has Daylight Savings Time (called Summer Time), which begins the last Sunday of March. It reverts to Standard Time the last Sunday in October.

Tipping

Tipping is acceptable and expected in Ireland. But be warned that if you give your customary 15% to 20% tip for outstanding service, you may in reality be giving over 35%. Many hotels and restaurants in Ireland automatically tack on a service charge of 10% to 15% to your room or meal.

It's customary to tip cab drivers around 10% (they don't automatically add it to the fare), more if the driver acts as a tour guide, filling you in on interesting tidbits of trivia about the sites you're passing. Porters should be tipped €1 per bag.

INDEX